D1525091

THE GEOGRAPHY OF ARRIVAL

THE GEOGRAPHY OF ARRIVAL

A memoir by George Sipos

GASPEREAU PRESS LIMITED

Printers & Publishers

2010

For my parents
Andrew & Elizabeth

Preface

At the beginning he is seven years old. He lives in a city
scarcely recovered from the War where bomb craters can
still be found among the buildings. People queue every
day in open-air markets to buy cabbages and bread. Men
in uniform stand in doorways at dusk.

One evening it is Christmas Eve. He is walking home
with his father and his mother from the twin-spired church
of the Cistercians. Along the way, his father reaches inside
his overcoat for a cigarette and discovers he has none left.
He hurries ahead to find a tobacconist still open at this
hour.

He and his mother follow through the darkening streets.
She walks more slowly than usual. Perhaps she is tired.
They reach their own gate, turn into it and climb the four
flights of stairs to the apartment. She unlocks the outside
door and stops in the vestibule. She looks at him with an air
of surprise and then turns toward the inner door. She has
heard something. It sounded like the rustling of garments,
or the beating of wings. From inside the room they hear a

bell tinkle. She draws him to her, and together they push the door inwards.

On a little table by the window, in a blaze of candlelight, a Christmas tree stands shimmering. He can smell the fragrance of evergreen and burning candles, see coloured glass sparkle, hear, or rather feel, the breath of departing wings.

He moves forward toward the tree. It doesn't occur to him to glance behind the door. He is lost in the miracle.

Suddenly his father is there, grumbling about how far he had to walk to find a tobacconist, and then he too catches sight of the tree. His mouth hangs open. He is amazed. The angels have come, just like when he was a boy. The three of them kneel around the tree. His father begins to sing the first hymn of Christmas:

> *The angel of the Lord has come down from heaven*
> *To bid the shepherds hasten to Bethlehem.*

Beyond the window, the angels move from street to street stirring the air with their wings. Tonight there are no tanks in the squares. Machine-gun fire is not heard in the distance. It is still ten months till crowds waving flags will march toward Parliament. The housewives who will be shot in the market, the teenagers with their gasoline bombs, the teachers with pickaxes who will dig up cobblestones for barricades are at home tonight.

They are singing by candlelight. Each room in the

benighted city is filled with the fragrance of burning candles.

After it is all over, he is again walking at twilight. His
mother holds his hand. It is early December and snow fills
the streets of the small town. Kind people dressed in heavy
coats speak to them in German.

The refugee camp is by the railway tracks, behind a row
of poplars. The buildings are warm and clean. They share
a room with eight other people. One is a stonemason who
goes into town to drink and comes back late and snores all
night.

They have passes to come and go as they please in the
town. His mother takes him every morning to the post
office. She is waiting for a letter from Canada. Each day they
stop outside the large windows of an automobile show-
room. Two cars are on display inside. One is low-slung
and white. The other pale blue with white seats. A circle of
chrome around a narrow three-pointed star glistens above
the square radiator. He learns his first words of German:
"Mercedes Benz."

Two days before they will leave the town, he and his
mother are walking through the streets beyond the mar-
ketplace. It is snowing. In the light of a street lamp he sees a
man in a fur hat pulling an evergreen tree behind him in the

snow. They stop. The man enters the gate of a large house. He drags the tree up the front steps, opens the door, and disappears inside.

"What was that man doing?" he asks his mother. "Why was he taking a tree into his house?" For a while she does not answer. They stand in the street with snow falling silently around them. Then she tells him: It was not the angels who brought their Christmas tree. People paid for their trees and dragged them home themselves through the streets. It was his father who had rung the bell and then hidden behind the door.

As they walk back to the camp, they pass through a square where a statue of a man with a beard and a peaked cap holds a walking stick up into the air. At the top of the stick is an old boot. Snow has mounded on its heel and sole. Above it there is nothing to be seen except dark flakes falling from the sky.

Christmas, when it comes, comes at sea. Years later he will learn an English carol about three ships that come sailing in on Christmas Day in the morning, but this ship is sailing out, past Gibraltar into the grey North Atlantic.

The last landfall was Ceuta in Spanish Morocco. They had all been allowed to go ashore for three hours. Those who did not seek out the bars of the port district wandered about under the palm trees of the residential quarter. He looked for camels and Arabs but all he saw was shacks of corrugated tin leaning against each other in the bright African sun. After a time a crowd of black-haired boys in white collarless shirts hounded them back to the port demanding cigarettes.

Now the ship lurches among the waves of the Atlantic. Passengers line up outside toilets, hang on to railings or sway against each other as the ship groans and creaks around them. The Italian crew, looking only slightly less miserable, come and go with buckets and mops.

In the dining room they have stopped laying the tables with the decanters of red wine and sparkling silverware that had accompanied meals on the first two days out of Genoa. The steward with the thin moustache and pink cheeks who had called him *bambino* and brought him extra dishes of ice cream stays in the galley holding on to a pillar and looking forlornly out a porthole.

On a table in the lounge near the dining room the crew have set up a little Nativity creche. A stable nestles on a bed of straw. Plaster-of-paris shepherds, oxen and sheep gather round, looking in while a brown Joseph and blue Mary kneel facing the manger. Because it is not yet Christmas, the manger is empty. An angel carrying a scroll perches on the roof of the stable.

Since Gibraltar, the various figures in the Nativity scene have been falling over with the increasing violence of the storm. Even the sheep are unable to keep their equilibrium and sprawl about in the chaos of straw. Occasionally a crew member sets the figures upright, but soon they tumble again, the sea rendering even the Three Wise Men merely human.

On the morning of Christmas Eve a pump gives out on the lowest deck. He and the other people from his cabin are evacuated through ankle-deep water to a lounge on an upper deck. All day the storm tosses the ship. In the afternoon someone says that they are passing the Azores but there is nothing to see out the windows but grey spray blown from the crests of waves.

That evening the pump is still not working and they bed down in the lounge where they have spent the day. They sleep as best they can.

Near morning, although it is still dark and although the ship still rises and falls with the waves, he leaves his bed. He holds on to chairs and posts and makes his way forward. When he reaches the end of the lounge he sees the Nativity scene.

Mary and Joseph, the shepherds and the Wise Men and all the animals lie scattered. Even the angel has toppled from the roof, the scroll across his chest like fallen masonry pinning him to the ground.

But then he looks inside the stable.

A baby Jesus is lying in the manger looking out at him. Someone from the crew has come in the night and tucked him in, ready for Christmas morning. Jesus has blue eyes and doesn't look the least bit seasick. He rides the waves as if he were in a little boat, heading confidently toward dawn.

They look at each other. Around them Mary and Joseph, the passengers and crew, the plaster angel lie tumbled. The ship plows westward toward Halifax.

In his manger, Jesus holds two little arms up in the air. He looks as if he were conducting music, or walking a tightrope. Years later he will hold his arms so to cure the sick, to bring back the dead, and to still the waters.

But he has just been born. For now, keeping his balance is enough.

1

Archaeology

The first and only time I visited Eldon House was a few weeks before leaving London for good.

I always knew it was there, that icon of Upper Canadian gentility, focus of antiquarian pride in the Anglo-Saxon world that was London. White and unprepossessing from Ridout Street, onto which it turned its back, the house faced the river across tumbling gardens and a steep treed bank. It was a well-known landmark, but no school had ever taken us on a field trip to gape at the history lessons in its chandeliers or its burnished wainscoting. And however much it may have been a municipal museum open to all, I would never have thought to just go in myself for a look, any more than I would have ventured through the Anglican doors of St. Paul's Cathedral, or than my mother would have asked to join the IODE.

There was an occasional item about Eldon House on the television news—a re-enacted soiree in period costume attended by the mayor, or a box of antique china donated to the museum by the estate of someone important recently deceased. And once, a newspaper article about a summer student who, while doing some kind of digging in the basement, broke through a bulkhead and discovered a hitherto unknown set of foundations. There he was in the photograph on his hands and knees, shovel in hand, pointing at a low section of stonework. It wasn't clear, either from the photograph or in the minds of the curators, what the find meant, but evidently it pointed to some architectural mystery from a forgotten episode in the house's history.

I was very taken by this discovery. I didn't mind that it was not a skeleton they had found, or a stash of cannonballs, or a Huron version of the Rosetta stone. The find was only a stone wall, but it had remained hidden all those years, down under the floorboards of that smug little museum.

It must have been about this time that the sewer line connecting our house to the main pipe under Piccadilly Street got plugged. A man came out and dug down beside the driveway till he found a clean-out where he could insert the long wire snake of his trade. I watched what came out: matted hair, half-dissolved tissue, and then a big lump of something containing three metal bottle caps—*Canada Dry Ginger Ale*—caught in a glob of hair and muck. The man shook his head and dropped the lump into his bucket. I knew what he was thinking. He glanced at me standing beside him: foreign little kid with ears sticking out and blue jeans rolled up above leather sandals. But he was wrong. I knew it must have been old Mr. McEwan our landlord who had flushed them down the toilet.

When friends of my parents who were moving to Florida told us about the upstairs apartment, Mr. McEwan wanted particularly to examine me before agreeing to rent. I sat on a footstool in the stillness of his parlour while my parents struggled with their English to answer his questions. There was a bottle of ginger ale on the sideboard and I was eventually offered a glass. I said *Please* and *Thank You* and kept the glass in my lap to avoid leaving rings on the furniture.

Evidently I passed muster because we moved in and lived upstairs for three years.

It was a nice apartment but I was disappointed to discover that the floors were completely level. We had stayed the previous winter, our first after arriving in Canada, in four dingy rooms shared with my uncle downtown. Through some result of the age of the building, all the floors sloped at peculiar angles. I could release a marble at the foot of my parents' bed and it would roll straight toward the door, without any need of an initial push or flick of a finger. Once at the door it took a sharp swerve to the left, caught the jamb on the hinge side and headed off down the hall, weaving gently from side to side. A quick bounce off the baseboard sent it into the kitchen where it swept in a wide arc across the linoleum to fetch up always at the same spot against the chipped enamel of the stove.

I had four marbles: three cat's-eyes and a small murky

green one. They had come in a box of cornflakes toward the end of our stay at my uncle's.

The first thing we had found in the cornflakes was a hockey player, a mystery that had us puzzled for weeks.

I was pouring out the last of the first box of cornflakes we had ever bought in Canada, and out tumbled a little red plastic hockey player. He was bent over from the waist and rested his stick horizontally above his knees. The face wasn't well enough defined to make out an expression, and in any case excess plastic which squeezed out between the halves of the mould had produced a flat growth between his nose and forehead, like an escaped gill, but it was clear from the attitude of readiness in his shoulders and upper body that he was waiting for the puck to be dropped, there among the flakes.

My father stopped eating. I picked the hockey player up and placed him upright in the middle of the table. We stared at him in silence. He stood there balanced on his skates, waiting.

"How do you suppose he got in the cornflakes?" I asked.

My father didn't reply. He went back to eating his breakfast but kept his eyes on the man and his stick.

It wasn't until suppertime that he had an answer: "It must have been one of the workers at the factory where they put the cornflakes into boxes. He has a little boy at home and he brought one of his toys with him to work by mistake, perhaps in the pocket of his shirt. The toy fell out and dropped into the box."

That made sense.

In any case I liked my hockey player. I stood him on the chest of drawers, and on the radio, and on the windowsill. I looked at him at eye-level. He was by himself but he didn't seem to mind. He stood there on his skates in front of the frost on the window and waited for the puck. His concentration wasn't broken by the fact that some kid somewhere might be missing him.

My father's theory held up until the next box of cornflakes. This time it was a blue hockey player who tumbled from the bottom of the box into my bowl. He had his stick level with his skates, on the forehand, and he was keeping his head up, looking for the pass.

We puzzled over this, my father and I, for three days. One clumsy workman maybe, but this was America. Such carelessness couldn't be endemic.

Then we made a discovery. There was a picture of a hockey player on the cornflakes box, and some writing. We couldn't understand what it said, but the conclusion was inescapable: The hockey players were in the boxes on purpose. There was nothing random or haphazard at work but an intentional benevolence, a treat for boys who ate up all their cornflakes.

"America!" was all my father had to say.

I started opening the boxes from the bottom, with a knife for the cardboard and scissors for the waxed paper. And there they were, one after the other, lying on the flakes like sunbathers on a beach. Before long I had five of them.

A full line, except for a goalie. That was the point at which they changed to marbles.

My next toy was a 1953 Pontiac. It was parked (or perhaps abandoned) in the courtyard at the back of the building. This was not so much an actual courtyard as a light well, surrounded by the backsides of brick buildings. An archway just wide enough for a car to pass through led to the back street. The only windows opening onto the vertical space of the well must have belonged to bathrooms because they were all opaque. A fire escape zigzagged down one wall, and several back doors opened onto a wooden porch usually piled with boxes of garbage. The Pontiac took up most of what space remained in the courtyard.

I first found the car after a big snowfall. At first it was just several indistinct mounds in the grey daylight filtering down from three stories up. I was wearing my new snow boots and mitts. In the silence of that place I started to brush away the snow from the hood of the car. I had never done anything like this before, but even so I knew that the secret was to do it slowly, a little at a time. The first thing that appeared was the topmost feathers of a headdress, and then a headband, and then a forehead.

This was a new kind of discovery—not a plastic toy in a box but shining metal, stern and substantial. Hockey players I had seen on TV, but an Indian chief emerging from outlines of snow, now that was something else. It combined with the solemnity of the place—the sombre walls, the smell of old grease, snow covering everything, the world beyond the archway unseen from this angle. And above all, the metallic precision of the chrome hood-ornament revealed bit by bit, and then the hood itself, the curve of the grill, headlights. Each sweep of a mitt and more metal emerged from beneath snow. What had already been revealed got elaborated, a coherent thing emerging from supposition.

I visited the Pontiac after every snowfall, and after every snowfall played out the quiet ritual of revelation. The mystery lay not in not knowing what the removal of snow would uncover, but in the archaeological act itself: the stern Indian chief always first, and then the rest of his monument.

Through the archway and several buildings down the street was a toothbrush factory where my mother worked for a while. It was a Dickensian sweatshop full of moulding and stamping machines for the production of toothbrushes that could be customized with dentists' names on the handles. For much of the time she worked there, my mother fed blank toothbrushes into a sinister stamping machine, though as occasional relief she also spent time in quality control snipping uneven bristles from finished brushes with a little pair of curved scissors. From time to time the stamping machine went askew and the dentist's name ended up crooked on the handle. On these occasions, my mother would come home with a box of defective brushes and we gave them to all our friends. For years ex-refugees across the city cleaned their teeth with the brushes of crooked dentists. It became a little ethnic joke.

The foreman at the toothbrush factory was a cheerful Lithuanian who amused the ragtag group of immigrant women under his charge by speculating about what would happen when Western civilization came to an end. Surely people would have to turn to cannibalism. So which among his little troupe of workers would make the best meal, he speculated, be the tastiest morsel? One week it would be this woman, the next another. My mother just couldn't enter into the spirit of his little fun. She came home one Wednesday on the verge of tears. Apparently it was her turn to be eaten.

"It's so awful," she said. "All day, every time I put a toothbrush into the machine, all I could think of was his teeth and his little moustache."

I was eighteen when I finally visited Eldon House. We had our tickets for the train to Vancouver and would be leaving as soon as school ended. I must have been revisiting scenes of my childhood before leaving London for good, though why I should go to Eldon House I can't think. Our old building downtown with its Bartleby-like courtyard still stood, although my uncle had long since moved. But it was to Eldon House I went.

The museum is impressive enough. Good furniture, pleasantly proportioned rooms. Not Wilton House or Petworth, but grand in its own way. The rooms speak of privilege and period elegance. A very nice dining room where the table is set as for a formal dinner with good china, silver and sparkling decanters. In the entrance hall an elephant's foot umbrella stand—a standard colonial accoutrement but the first such I had ever seen. I couldn't shake the thought that this tame receptacle of umbrellas and walking sticks had once been attached to a real elephant, one foot of four keeping the hulking, snow-covered Pontiac of a beast in who knows what foreign country upright.

They had marked out the whole house with rope cordons and red runners indicating the route visitors were to take through the rooms.

By this time I had forgotten the story of the mysterious foundations. But in one of the bedrooms I reached into my pocket and discovered what was no longer there, and had not been for a long time. But if I had found it, if I had had a marble, and if I had put it down at the head of a red runner, I knew without a doubt the route it would take on its journey through the house. And I knew, here at the end of things, where it would come to rest.

Loupe

The city block at the northeast corner of Dundas and Ridout Streets, which is now the windowless and grey monolith of the Provincial Court building, was, in 1957, a Hopper-esque stretch of two-storey shopfronts in honey-coloured brick. I don't remember now what was on the corner itself, but next to it, just east along the north side of Dundas, a modest greasy-spoon called the Panama Restaurant belonged, in the year we arrived in Canada, to my father's brother who had come here after the War via a factory in Bradford. It was the kind of diner where mashed potatoes were served with an ice-cream scoop onto plates of liver-and-onions. A mural depicting green hills on either side of a waterway, presumably the Panama Canal, covered the back wall. The waitress wore a black blouse and skirt and a little white apron. Soon after we arrived I was treated here to my first American dessert: a banana split. My uncle produced it himself, in a long glass dish with a banana cut in half, three scoops of ice-cream and a cherry. I had never seen anything like it before, and for many years it defined

for me the country we had come to—cold, rich, extrava-
gantly assembled.

My uncle lived above the restaurant in the apartment
with crooked floors and tall windows that leaked cold air
in winter. He and his Greek wife had one room and my
grandmother had another, she having emigrated in 1953.
For a time after our arrival in Canada we lived there too, my
parents sleeping on a pullout sofa and I on a cot. It was here
my father and I learned to watch hockey on the television.
I was about to say on the "antique" television, but there
were no such things then—all televisions were new. It is
only in hindsight that the wood-grained metal cabinet and
its curved glass screen that looked like the porthole of an
ocean liner seem ancient. When the fans in Detroit threw
their hats, or even the occasional octopus, onto the ice
after each monochrome Red Wings' goal, there was nothing contrived, nothing self-referential or retro about the
medium. Their exuberance and excess, like the optimism of
the era as a whole, was really happening somewhere among
the wintry streets of Detroit. Television then was about
simple belief and joy. Semiology would come later. In the
same way for my uncle, the Panama Restaurant was about
moving on to something obviously better than the disaster
of Europe.

A few doors east along Dundas Street was a modest Loblaws. I'm amazed now that there should have been such a
thing in the middle of the block, tucked in like a clothing
store or a stationers, without a parking lot and without the

architectural ostentation we have since come to associate
with supermarkets. But there it was. The first photograph
my parents took with the Kodak box camera somebody
had given them was of my mother holding up a pineapple
in the produce section. I think she chose it because she had
no idea what it was. They sent copies of the photograph to
relatives back home to whom it was meant as proof we were
alive and happy in a country inexplicable though abundant.
It was at this Loblaws too that my parents bought a card-
table and four folding chairs which served as our dining
furniture for many years. Also an oil-painting of an Italian
landscape in an elaborate frame.

At the eastern end of the block, on Talbot Street, a Hungarian of my parents' acquaintance owned a tiny jewellery
store where he repaired watches. He had a blonde wife who
my parents said "put on airs" because her father had been
a military officer between the wars, and because she had
ambitions for her husband, even if he didn't. Left to himself, he would have been happy to spend his days bent over
his workbench, a jeweller's loupe screwed into his eye and
a rack of tiny tools ready to hand. In the end, however, she
prevailed and within a year of our arrival they left for Los
Angeles. We heard later that they opened a shop in a ritzy
neighbourhood under a fake aristocratic version of their
surname and became wealthy.

Before they left, the jeweller gave me some of his old
tools—two tiny screwdrivers, a pair of tweezers, and a loup
with a cracked frame. It was too big for my eye and I could

only wear it for short intervals, but I used it and the screw-drivers to take apart an old alarm clock he had also given me. I spread the little cogs and spindles on the tabletop and looked at them, one eye shut and the other wedged open with the loupe. The fine machined pieces smelled lightly of oil and seemed bigger than life through the glass. They were like the workings of a foreign world.

The Loblaws and the restaurant and the stores are now gone, but a few of the old buildings on Dundas Street remain, from which it is possible to extrapolate some of what has vanished—the worn brick and the second-storey windows lit after dark, the lives going on inside, marking time.

3

Rabbit

For a long time Gibbons Park provided the only easy public access to the banks of the North Thames. It occupied a bench of low land between the escarpment to the east and a long bend of the river north of Blackfriars Bridge. A paved walkway followed the river, and there were playing fields and picnic grounds and a haphazard arboretum of various kinds of maple, poplar, willow and ornamental spruce.

The park was a favoured place for school picnics, foot races, watermelon-eating contests and all the other communal pleasures of a world that predated jogging and tai chi. After one school picnic, when we were done with the games and sports and miniature tubs of vanilla ice cream and their little wooden spoons, we piled onto the school bus for the trip back to St. Michaels. Someone started up "Ninety-nine Bottles of Beer on the Wall." By the time the bus pulled up in front of the school we were down to nine, and everyone stayed on till we got rid of them all—a busfull of kids going nowhere, singing at the tops of our treble voices.

I remember two things about Gibbons Park that complicate, in a peculiar way, such easy nostalgia. The first was a field house near the river. Whether it was merely a shed for storing lawnmowers and other Parks Board equipment, or some kind of sports pavilion or change house for a swimming pool about whose existence my memory is uncertain, I can't say. But I remember distinctly a low stucco building with a red roof and high windows permanently closed behind green shutters. A large weeping willow trailed branches against the stucco and cast a moving screen of leaf-shadow across the ochre walls.

I wouldn't have known to call the walls ochre until years later, and that's the curious thing about it. Even then I remembered little about my early childhood in Hungary, and it wouldn't be till much later that I discovered the particular yellows and faded pinky-golds of Eastern European buildings. But the shadow of willow leaves on that wall evoked a nostalgia and feeling of exoticism I couldn't possibly explain. When I bought a camera in my early teens, I spent whole afternoons taking photographs of those shadows on the wall. The pictures were always a disappointment, of course. What was missing was movement, and the ability to capture time not frozen by the click of the shutter but in the evanescent act of its elapsing. The pang of that wall and its green windows, the restless swish of leaves and their insubstantial shadows were more real for me, for a time, than anything I believed I could ever know in the city above the escarpment.

Not far from this field house, behind a yew hedge, there was also a tiny formal garden. It had been built to com-memorate someone or something, but I have no idea what. A clipped hedge of box perhaps ten-feet square enclosed an ornamental pool into which a stone cherub poured a steady, pencil-thin stream of water from an urn resting on his hip. Even I could see the conventionality of this garden, and it took only a step or two behind the statue to reveal the electric pump and plumbing that kept the whole thing going. But for all that, the garden epitomized for me the concept of classical elegance, again at a time when I had no idea what "the classical" as a historic aesthetic might mean. But I know that years later when I visited the Boboli Gar-dens in Florence I immediately recognized everything. Not as: "So this is what the pool and hedge and kid in Gibbons Park were pale imitations of," but more as if I had been here before, as if the fragrance of box in that London park, the formalism of water pouring from stone had been a remem-brance of something I would experience only years later, not as a premonition, recognized as such in hindsight, but a genuine remembrance, like the dunking of a madeleine into coffee.

I usually reached Gibbons Park via the end of Grosvenor Street. From its intersection with St. George at the top of the escarpment, Grosvenor ran sharply downhill to a gravel parking lot near the south end of the park. On the right was a row of houses, and on the left a high-rise apartment building. Between this high-rise and the park below was a piece of undeveloped scrubland of bushes, small trees and the usual undergrowth of uncared-for places.

In the summer this pocket of scrub was impenetrable, but in winter you could squeeze between the bare branches. I discovered one year that the snow inside was criss-crossed with rabbit tracks, two long and two short footprints for each jump, just the way my library books had shown. Although the place was a long way from home, I decided I would try to catch one of the rabbits in a trap. On a Saturday in March I took the bus and transported the necessary equipment to the rabbit-infested bush: a small wooden box, a stick and a carrot. I found a good spot well inside the thicket where there were plenty of tracks, propped the box up on the stick, and put the carrot underneath.

It never occurred to me to wonder how the trap was meant to be triggered, nor what any rabbit I might succeed in catching would do inside the box during the week that elapsed till I could go and check what had happened. Years later when I came across Dürer's famous woodcut I supposed that that might have been how I had imagined my rabbit looking, waiting calmly in the dark. The truth is, I expected almost anything else: to find the box still propped on its stick, the carrot frozen inside, or the box gone altogether, stolen by some other kid with different ideas. When I arrived, however, there it lay, flat on the ground on the exact spot where I had left it, the stick gone, the mouth of the box sealed by snow.

My first reaction was panic. What would I do if there were a rabbit inside? Let it go? Try to strangle it? Take it home? In what? I hadn't brought a thing with me, except my bus fare.

But I couldn't just walk away. I had set a trap and it had been sprung. That's not something you can simply ignore. In any case, there was a whole high-rise full of windows above the trees as witness.

I looked at the box. It sat there, small, squat, revealing nothing until I should slip my gloved fingers under the rim and look. I lifted the edge. No contented bunny wrinkled its nose inside. No frantic half-starved creature leapt through the crack toward freedom. The box was untenanted.

But equally … no carrot either.

An empty box then, but not a failure. Here was proof that *something* had happened. I had had an idea (a pretty dumb one, yes) and it had led to something: a box falling, a carrot vanished. An outcome both probable and yet unforeseen.

And if that could happen, what else might?

What else not?

4

Anchor

McMahon Pool, on the east side of Adelaide just north of the CPR tracks, was one of many rudimentary outdoor swimming pools in the city. It was a modest rectangle of concrete with a cement surround where bathers could lie in the sun within a chain-link fence topped with barbed wire. On the street side there was a brick change house with a Boy's door and a Girl's door leading to and from the pool through footbaths of disinfectant. The change-house walls listed the usual prohibitions: *No Running. No Pushing. No Diving. No Inflatable Toys.*

On hot summer days the pool was overcrowded with kids running, pushing each other into the deep end, and doing cannonballs into any square foot of unoccupied water they could see. Every hour the lifeguard blew her whistle, and all the swimmers had to climb out and sit on the edge with their feet in the water. She fetched a white jug and walked along behind the bathers pouring bleach into the pool above their heads. When the jug was empty, she blew her whistle again and everyone kicked their feet for a full minute to mix the bleach into the water. On the third whistle they were free to jump back in, which they did, several hundred at once. Any bacteria that could survive all that were welcome to it.

McMahon Pool was where I failed to learn to swim over the course of three years. The first two years were spent avoiding getting my face wet. Week after week I lowered myself into the shallow end, held on to the edge in line with the other students, stretched my feet out behind me as instructed and kicked. The only thing I could not do was lower my head between my arms and immerse my face below the churning surface. Sports pedagogy in those days relied heavily on abuse of the incompetent and also on the motivational effectiveness of hierarchies. While the other kids progressed quickly through the ranks of Ducks and Sharks and Motorboats, I remained for two years the sole occupant of the class where we had all begun—an Anchor.

Nevertheless, by my third summer I did somehow succeed in holding my head briefly underwater, achieved probably in a moment of inadvertence when nobody was splashing nearby and the instructor's attention was focussed elsewhere. The next hurdle, however, which occupied the whole of the third year, was to open my eyes underwater, a thing I could not possibly do. Apart from the chemical sting of the bleach, eyes were organs intended for air and light. Opening them in water would be like trying to breathe in a vacuum, or eat dirt, or set fire to your hair. How could anyone expect you to just do it, open your eyelids in a foreign medium as if elemental categories counted for nothing?

But in the end I managed even that. On the final day of lessons I stood in chest-deep water with the instructor beside me. He told me to immerse my head fully while he held his fist under water and extended several fingers. I was to look to see how many fingers he held out and then come to the surface and tell him. Somehow, I don't know how, I finally managed it; I opened my eyes in the green murk and looked for his fingers. Strangely, all that water pressing suddenly against my eyeballs didn't seem either alien or particularly unpleasant. And there were his fingers, four of them, blurry and waving in refracted light, but definitely countable. I burst through the surface in triumph: "Four! There were four fingers."

"Aw, you little cheat, you never looked—I had five." And so I remained an Anchor.

The conclusion my parents drew from this constant defeat was that what I needed were more lessons. They signed me up for the whole winter at the indoor pool at the YMCA. This provided an almost identical experience to the summer sessions at McMahon Pool, but with one difference. Since the class was all boys, about fifty of us, the instructor, a bald, bowlegged man with an earring and leathery skin, told us he wanted us to swim without bathing trunks. Technically, this meant we could go home in the howling blizzards of a London winter without worrying about wet bathing suits freezing. A more modern sensibility would, of course, suspect other motives.

None of the other boys seemed to mind, but for some reason I refused, and was the only one of the whole group who brought a bathing suit to each lesson. It wasn't just prudishness, though I'm sure that entered into it. It was more like the business of eyeballs and water. There were boundaries of the natural which seemed improper, not to say impossible, to cross. Never mind that the sight of forty-nine boys swimming happily in their birthday suits might have caused me to question what was natural and what was not. But give a boy of twelve, particularly one who has taken three years to become even marginally reconciled to the idea of water in his ears and eyes, a choice between Rousseau and Aquinas and it should be no surprise which way he'll go.

But at least I was no longer an Anchor. The bald instructor called me Blue Pants. I took this as progress, oblivious to his contempt. And in fact I did finally learn to do the Dead Man's Float, and then to kick my feet, and eventually to master an inelegant and utterly inefficient Australian Crawl. In time I could actually make it from one side of the pool to the other. The rest of the boys were swimming lengths by then, so my widths were not without hazard. But we all kept a tally of how far we had swum, added it up each week and marked our progress on a big map of Canada. By spring we had collectively made it halfway down the St. Lawrence.

As a prize (awarded about the time we reached Trois Rivieres) the YMCA took us on a bus trip to see a hockey game in Toronto. We left on a Saturday afternoon, dropped our sleeping bags at the Y on Yonge Street, and went straight to Maple Leaf Gardens. The other kids were excited. We sat way up at the top of the greys, from where seeing the game was just like watching it on TV except without the instant replays. As it turned out this didn't matter because there was nothing to replay. Toronto and Chicago played to a scoreless tie.

When the game was over they gave us two choices: we could either go downstairs to the hallway outside the dressing rooms to try to get players' autographs, or one of the chaperones could take us for a ride on the subway.

All the kids opted for the autographs except me. So while they pushed and shouted their way down the stairs into the nether regions of the arena, I set off with my adult guide to the subway station at the corner. We rode down an escalator, which I knew about because they had them in London at Simpson's, and then waited on a long dimly-lit platform. As the train approached, there was first a rush of sound and light from somewhere down a tube in the earth, followed by a strange rubbery wind. Then the train burst into view and slid to a stop with its windows and doors lit. People got off and on, and then we too were inside and the station turned into a blur and the darkness of the tunnel swallowed us and rushed by with its indistinct brickwork and pipes and wires waving outside. Who knew where we were headed, or what buildings or basements or sewers we were slipping under. All I knew was this was Toronto, the mythical city I had never seen before. I wasn't seeing it now either but was in it anyway, late at night, by myself (or close to it), rushing below the surface toward its unknown centre.

Which, when we got to it, turned out to be Union Station.

We emerged from the subway first by an escalator, then up a flight of stairs into the cavern of the departure hall, and then up more stairs to the street outside. Out in the night air taxis filled the whole length of the street, and cars and buses and people with suitcases came and went everywhere under the rows of street lights. What took my breath, however, what I could not have imagined before this moment, was the building opposite. A huge stone cliff stretched the full width of the block and disappeared upward into the darkness above the lights, higher than any building I had ever seen. Up in the sky a sign said *Royal York* in huge foreshortened letters. Below it, row on row of windows, lit or glowing, were so distinct I felt it would be nothing to reach out and touch them. I could see curtains drawn or pulled back, and lamps behind them all the way up and across the vast sweep of grey granite.

It was as if the night of the immense city were the most transparent thing I had ever looked through, the purest air. If I started to count—the windows, the lamps, the taxis on the street, the clear-edged particulars of this suddenly visible world—I knew I would get them all and not miss a single one.

5

Rocket

This starts the old-fashioned way, with a setting.

Imagine a square. Not abstract and seen from above, floating in an ideal Euclidian space, but approached from ground level with dirt underfoot. The southwest corner is where Harley Street runs into Victoria. From here, the southern edge of the square stretches east, following a little row of dull houses on the south side of Victoria, while opposite is an expanse of empty meadow. The western edge of the meadow is a row of poplars stretching north toward Huron Street. To the left of these trees the ground falls away to the backyards of houses on Leroy Avenue. You can't see Huron Street to the north because just short of the top edge of the square the meadow dips over a small escarpment leaving the eye to continue above the hidden road toward a line of trees in the distance along the river. To the east, the meadow is bounded by Barker Street and the dark wall of evergreens where St. Peter's Cemetery stretches all the way from Victoria to Huron.

Ten acres all told, possibly less. A bit of unfenced prairie—grass and goldenrod and daisies in summer. The meadow belongs to the Church and awaits expansion of the cemetery at some future date, but to our neighbourhood this ownership is purely notional. The meadow is used as common land for walking dogs, riding bicycles and flying kites, and for tobogganing at its north end in winter. For some of us it is a route to school. A dirt path leads from the southwest corner on a more or less straight diagonal to the northeast where St. Lawrence School sits on the lowland across Huron by the corner of the cemetery. Walking or riding our bicycles, we have every dip and rise of the path memorized.

As settings go, this is perhaps a humble one. It is not W.O. Mitchell's prairie, and is way too small to yield mythic encounters with death and transcendence. No gophers, no dugouts to provide a locus for rites of passage or to harbour idiot-savant veterans or Metis outcasts. Just a big field full of crickets and wind, with an Ontario sky overhead.

There was at one time a small gravel pit at the north-west corner where we played war—hid behind piles of dirt, ambushed each other, and practised dying with the theatrical gestures we had seen on TV. There was an apple tree there too, the last of an ancient orchard behind a der-elict farmhouse near the pit, and we did occasionally sneak through the weeds to steal some of its meagre fruit. But if there was any Edenic implication it was lost on us. We just wished the apples had tasted better, and that we had more caps for our guns.

Nor did we make much of the grave at the southeast

corner of the meadow. Somehow it had ended up on the wrong side of Barker Street, not in the fenced and shady confines of the cemetery but in the field itself, with a headstone low to the ground and a small bush at its foot. Maybe it predated the cemetery; maybe it was ahead of its time. Now that I live in British Columbia and am familiar with the straight line a forest makes at the edge of a cutblock, I am tempted to see this grave as something seeded by the cemetery across the road, like a bit of natural regen. But I saw no irony in it at the time. It was just a grave. We neither avoided it nor sought it out, just stumbled on it now and then.

My clearest memory is of trying to launch a rocket from the dead centre of the meadow. It was a red rocket, standing about a foot high, made of plastic with four curved fins. Here is how it was meant to work: You started by holding the rocket upside down and filling it with some sort of liquid whose identity I can no longer recall. Then you stuffed baking soda into a little plastic insert, screwed it into the tail of the rocket, turned the whole thing upside-right, and clamped it onto its launch pad. You lay down in the grass about ten feet away holding a piece of string and counted. The idea was that the chemical reaction between the baking soda and the liquid would create pressure in the rocket. If you pulled the string at just the right moment to release it from its launch pad, the rocket would streak up into the sky. The reason it was red was so you could keep it in sight among the clouds.

Of course it was a great disappointment. I either waited too long and pulled the string after the pressure had all leaked out and the rocket just sat there, or I pulled it too soon and it just flopped over onto its side in a little puddle of fizz. I tried often enough, but in the end the most fun I ever got out of that rocket was holding it in the air in my left hand as I pedalled my bike across the meadow making whooshing noises—to heck with the false promises of thrust.

I did, however, get it to work just once. I don't know how it happened but it actually took off and rose about twenty feet. But even this was a letdown. I had read my Robert A. Heinlein and knew that a rocket taking off should be a glorious thing—flames and smoke and a deep roaring, then a streak of fire across the sky. But all I got was a quick spurt like the cap coming off a pop bottle, and then a soundless rise and fall. It looked and felt no different than a ball thrown into the air, or a stone, or a clod of dirt.

When it fell back to the ground it just lay there—intact for sure, but also unscarred. I don't know what I expected, but I longed to see it pockmarked by a journey among stars, singed by the heat of re-entry—luminous, if possible, with the afterglow of galaxies. Instead it was merely a thing of earth returned to earth. A piece of plastic, innocuous and inconsequential among the daisies.

6

The Three Cs

The Colborne Community Centre was located between
Dundas and Queens on the west side of Colborne Street.
At one time it had been the Catholic Cultural Centre but
had changed its name, though not its initials, when ownership had passed from ecclesiastical into secular hands.

Under either dispensation, I don't remember anyone
ever referring to it other than as *The Three Cs*. For a long
time, since I only heard the place spoken of and never paid
attention to what was written above its facade, I thought
it was actually called *The Three Seas*, an odd abbreviation
of the legendary seven perhaps explainable by London's
landlocked location.

Not far from The Three Cs, possibly right next door
though my memory is hazy on this, was a house that had
been converted into the workshop and dispensary of a
medical technician who specialized in artificial eyes. He
had converted the front window into a showcase where
horizontal wooden racks held rows of glass eyeballs.
(Surely I can't be making this up. I remember clearly stand-

ing in front of the window looking at them, and the eyes staring back, not impassively perhaps, but with no more recognition or empathy than you might see in any crowd. They were only glass after all.)

My first visit inside The Three Cs, soon after our arrival in London, was to a Sunday service conducted by a minister of the Hungarian Reformed Church, of which my mother was then a member. This must have been in the days when the building was still owned by the Catholics, a piece of logic that seemed to amaze no-one at the time.

Later, I became quite familiar with the musty auditorium when I competed year after year in public speaking contests for students from across the city. I wonder now why I did it, got dressed in a suit and tie in Grades 6 and 7 and 8, to stand sweating in the wings while girls in dresses with bows at the waist went ahead of me, little notecards clutched in their cupped hands as they tried their darndest to be cute on the subject of *Procrastination*, or to address themselves with either real or mock-seriousness to the question: *Does Father Really Know Best?*

I should have hated it, but I didn't. My parents, of course, were inordinately proud that their son, who had known not a word of English three or four years earlier, won little gold pins for making speeches in public. I just liked walking out on a stage with the lights shining down, rows of people in the worn, plush seats, the judge with her notebook and stopwatch shadowy in the middle, and I with a bunch of words to say—the challenge of remembering them all and getting them right.

I'm sure my speeches were quite dreadful, as saccharine in their way as those of the pert girls. Mercifully, I remember only one of them. It was called *Mysteries of the Sea*, and was a rather pointless compilation of facts about odd sea creatures I had read about in an encyclopedia at the London Public Library. What else could it have been? London, as I say, was irredeemably landlocked, and the few glimpses I had caught of the North Atlantic between bouts of seasickness on our crossing to Halifax hardly constituted personal experience of marine biology.

The only creature I now remember talking about was the sea cucumber. It was the one part of my speech I didn't worry about getting right. I stood there with my feet planted on the stage, looked out at all the other kids' parents looking back at me, and told them what I knew:

The sea cucumber is about six inches tall. When it is threatened, it vomits up its insides. While its attackers are busy eating these, the sea cucumber escapes, hides in a quiet place, and grows a new set of organs. That it can do this over and over is truly one of the many mysteries of the sea.

Industrial Arts

Across the street from my high school, on the southwest corner of Colborne and Queens, stood one of the fine old brick mansions that had in an earlier age graced the tree-lined streets of central London.

The Church had acquired the house at some point and turned it into an annex of the school. The lovely high-ceilinged living and dining rooms on the main floor had been converted into industrial-education workshops. Fluorescent lights had replaced chandeliers, and lathes, drill presses and workbenches covered the hardwood floors. A separate door from the porch led, by way of an unseen staircase, to rooms above where Home Economics was taught to the girls. Presumably upstairs was full of sewing machines and stoves, though it was a separate universe about which I could only conjecture. After lunch on Thursdays our Grade 9 class marched across the street, and girls and boys vanished through the appropriate doors into our own segments of the ark.

The key to what those afternoons among the workbenches and machines meant may lie in the fact that in those days what we were doing was called not *Shop* but *Industrial Arts*. It may have been a training for industry, but more importantly it was an initiation into art—an education, however consciously or unconsciously understood, of the senses. What I remember is the fragrance of sanded fir, the soft thunk of a mallet on the splayed handle of a chisel, the way wood-glue squeezed out into little pearls from between boards clamped in a vise, the rising whine of an electric motor when it was turned on, shavings spinning like eyelashes from the lathe.

And it was not just about the senses, but about a sense of craft also, however little we understood it, or however poorly we mastered even the simplest tasks: The way a plane judders against the grain, but slips smoothly with it. The way oil smokes from the bit when you've applied it just right on the drill press. How tools can make the hand awkward or graceful.

God knows what the girls did upstairs. Sewed blouses perhaps, or baked cookies. Whatever occupied their afternoons in the feminine empyrean, surely it could only have been utilitarian—an economy, after all, and not an art. We tried to make useful things too: pipe racks, cheeseboards, plumb bobs—but that was never the real point. The point was the ritual of tools and technique, of material and its transformations, of the ethics and aesthetics of the creative act.

At least that's one version of the story.

Here is another:

Our Industrial Arts teacher, Mr. Kersley, a rosy-cheeked former mill-worker from the Midlands who loved to tell stories of gruesome industrial accidents involving severed limbs and spectacular plunges into vats of boiling chemicals, was also a passionate amateur of art history. He owned a huge collection of slides of paintings from the Renaissance right through to Abstract Expressionism. He found many occasions to show them to us, and not just for the obvious benefits to be gained by adolescent boys from representations of unclothed female anatomy. He talked about light and the Impressionists, about the promise and eventual dead end of Cubism, about Dada.

The slide I remember most is of Munch's *The Scream*, the twisted lines of the face and its framing hands, the way the entire landscape becomes part of whatever anguish consumes the soul of the subject.

I thought of this painting often as I worked on my major project for the course. For some reason, instead of building something useful and complicated out of wood or metal, I had decided to saw a piston from an automobile engine in half. I think I had an idea of how illuminating it would be to see the piston in cross-section, with the connecting rod dangling from whatever pivot might be inside. And so hour after hour, I worked away at the thing with a hacksaw, the blade shrieking back and forth through the piston head. I hated the thing pretty soon, but couldn't stop. All I would have had then would have been a half-mutilated piston instead of something revealed.

And so I stuck with it, that endless back and forth till my arm ached and the blade got hot and needed to be replaced. It took weeks, but I did succeed. There, finally, were the two halves, looking like parts of a hollow Easter egg, or like a heart sliced open.

The inside of the piston was remarkably dull: a hollow space, a small shaft for the connecting rod, nothing much else. Unlike the outer surfaces, which had been machined smooth, the inside was black and rough as if forged in some brutal fire.

Whatever else, I certainly learned about obsession and futility, and a thing or two about the toughness of steel. Also that craft has little to do with heroism, and everything with the dumb stubbornness of substance.

8

$CaCl_2$

At its western end, York Street crosses Ridout and heads downhill to a bridge over the south branch of the Thames. Once across, the road carries on as Stanley Street, one of those transformations that is not uncommon in Europe but is unusual in Canadian cities. But at least the river marks a clear boundary between one name and the other.

On the south side of York, just before it dips to the river, is Copps Building Supply. It has been in this location for at least fifty years, a stone's throw from the old Middlesex Courthouse and the site of the first habitation of London.

The only time I ever bought anything at Copps was in the spring of my final year in high school.

We had studied the famous Cavendish experiment in Chemistry about how the chemical composition of water can be determined by synthesizing it from hydrogen and oxygen. Perhaps the year was coming too quickly to an end, or perhaps the school didn't have enough of the appropri-

ate glassware, but there were no plans for us actually to con-
duct the experiment. We were to make do with diagrams
and an explanation in our textbook. Maybe for the same
reason, that the year was too quickly ending—and with
it my years in high school, my time in London and possibly much else besides—I decided that I would do the
experiment myself after school. It was an era when institu-
tional liability was much less on anyone's mind and nobody
seemed to object so long as I promised not to burn the
place down and to leave before the janitors finished their
shift.

The experiment involved an apparatus like an oversized
oil lamp containing zinc chips in one glass sphere and
dilute sulphuric acid in the other. The acid acted on the
zinc to produce hydrogen gas. By measuring the mass of
hydrogen produced in this generator, combining it with air,
passing the resulting water vapour through a condensation
coil, capturing the condensate in a flask and then weigh-
ing it, you could determine, as had Henry Cavendish in
the eighteenth century, how many atoms of hydrogen and
oxygen make up a molecule of water. In order to capture
all the synthesized water so it could be weighed, the flask
needed to contain a quantity of calcium chloride.

All this seemed straightforward enough, except that
the school did not possess any $CaCl_2$. I had never thought
to wonder where scientific substances came from. When
we needed carbon tetrachloride, our teacher produced a
bottle of it from a storage room. When frogs or crickets

were to be dissected, they appeared neatly chloroformed and injected with dyes. Once in Grade 9 when we were studying the parts of the buttercup we were stunned when Sister Chrysostom plunked down a whole bouquet of them on her desk. She had asked the driver of the bus that brought the nuns from the convent to the school to stop so she could climb down to the ditch and pick an armful of the yellow weeds for the day's class. It had never occurred to us that our black and white line diagrams of stamen and pistil and calyx had anything to do with actual plants growing in the real world.

So where to get calcium chloride? All I knew was that it was a white powder that was supposed to come in a jar. It was too late in the year to ask the school to order some from a scientific supply company. Somebody somewhere in London must sell the stuff, but where and why? Calcium chloride's main property was to absorb water, so who, apart from a scientist, would want to absorb water with a powder? What was wrong with a sponge? Then somebody told me that they had heard there was something you could sprinkle on concrete if you had a wet basement. So to a building supply store. So to Copps.

When I bicycled down to York and Ridout they said yes ideed, they sold it in twenty-pound bags. But I only needed about fifty grams. And I only had a few dollars. Nor did we have a problem with a damp basement at home on which I could use the rest of a bag. In any case we were moving to Vancouver in a few months. But they found a solution for

me. They had had a broken bag sitting in the back somewhere for some time and I was welcome to as much of it
as I wanted.

Except that the one main property of calcium chloride
is to absorb water. The broken bag had been doing just that
for several months and the powder had hardened into a
solid lump. But the Copps people, helpful again, found
a hammer and we whacked away at the mass till a chunk
broke off. All I would have to do, they said, is grind it up
somehow and heat it to evaporate most of the water. It
would be good as new.

So that's what I set out to do. I ground up the chunk of
rock in a mortar and pestle and then put the damp powder
into a ceramic crucible and set it above a Bunsen burner.
Soon a liquid formed in the bottom of the crucible. A few
minutes later it started to bubble. Ten minutes later it was
still bubbling. Twenty minutes later still. Oddly, instead
of the liquid decreasing in volume and leaving a dry white
powder, the contents of the crucible was all liquid by now.
Could it be that I had long ago stopped evaporating water
and had melted the calcium chloride itself? After all, everything had a melting point. And if so, when had I crossed the
boundary between one process and the other? And how
could I have told the difference?

More to the point, what was I to do now? How to go
back to the beginning? If I simply turned off the gas, surely
the liquid would harden into a solid lump even more use-
less than what I had started with, and perhaps even fuse to

the crucible for good. But if I kept going, where would it end?

All around me the glass apparatus of the wonderful experiment gleamed in the late afternoon sun—the hydrogen generator, the distillation coil, the neat beakers and flasks. It was all as the textbook diagrams indicated. But something had gone wrong. A piece of the real world, a rock, had led me astray, tempted me across an invisible boundary and now left me stuck.

Light flooded the football field outside the window. Inside everything was still except for the Bunsen burner and its soft rush of gas, a flame that seemed to me, as I stared into it, bluer and swifter than any river.

9

Dipping Bird

In the spring of Grade 12, a group of four or five students from my high school went to have tea with a 92-year-old woman who lived in one of the high-rise apartment buildings just outside the university gates along Richmond Street. We had only a vague idea of who she was—a famous scientist who had done something important in her day—but the reason behind our visit was clear. We were doing a good deed for a nice old lady by listening to her talk about her life in science. And we were also meant to be inspired by a real scientist serving us cookies and tea from porcelain cups to seek lives of academic curiosity and endeavour. Needless to say, the visit was not our idea.

Our science teacher, Sister Celestine, had come up with the notion of sending us on this excursion as a perfect way of combining benevolence toward a distinguished retired scientist (who may well have been her teacher at one time, their ages being about right) and a useful way of demystifying the scientific life for a group of students she saw as having potential. It would have been entirely consistent with her character to have thought it out just so, like measuring out how many moles of this you would have to add to that to achieve a given exothermic reaction. She was a committed teacher. Her dominant tic, which students learned to mimic, mostly with affection, was her deliberate and calculated mispronunciation of scientific words. She called fluorine, for instance, "flu-o-rine," emphatically inserting two vowels in the middle of the word, with a second accent on the "o," not because she thought this was the right way to say it, nor because she expected us or anyone else to pronounce it so, but to ensure that any students she taught would, for the rest of their lives, be able to spell the word correctly.

Would anyone other than a nun have done this, sacrificed technical truth, risked ridicule even, in the interest of what she saw as a higher calling? Possibly the nice old lady with the cookies. She had received her PhD from Bryn Mawr in 1901, we found out, and then spent the twentieth century, or as far as we had got in it, at various universities doing research in physics. She retired to London in 1940 and then promptly unretired once she found out that important work was going on at Western on the development of radar for the war effort. As far as we could gather, she worked for free for the next dozen years till she was almost 80. And as far as we could gather also from the absence of framed photographs in her living room of children or grandchildren, or indeed any photographs at all, she had remained single all her life, devoting herself to her own higher calling.

As a role model, she had an uncertain effect on us. She was intelligent, well-spoken and charming, but we, not surprisingly, had other notions about the ideal life. For my part, I had difficulty listening to, let alone understanding, her explanation (watered down God knows how much for our benefit) of her work on the reflectivity of microwave radiation, absorbed as I was in the way sunlight caught the golden hair of the girl across the room. Absorbed by how different the geometry of her body looked as she leaned on the armrest of a sofa from the way I was accustomed to observing her two rows to my right in Math and French. Watching always, then as now, for a glance in return.

Purpose. Method. Observations. Conclusions. As a way of proceeding, science left much to be desired. But if you added faith, or desire—the purity of some kind of conviction or obsession—what then?

In lieu of photographs, the coffee table and windowsills were covered with a collection of ingenious physics toys. In one, two antique wooden men held opposite ends of a saw and drew it back and forth across a log in response to what hidden source of energy based on what physical principle I can no longer recall. Our host took delight in demonstrating these toys and asking us to try to explain how they might work. The one I do remember well was a glass bird. It had a bulbous body and a thin tube for a neck joining it to an oversized head. The whole thing pivoted on a stand and for no apparent reason the bird would periodically tip forward, dip its beak into a glass of water, and then return to an upright position.

Did our host explain its action, or did I read about it years later? I do know now that the secret is in the felt feathers on the bird's head. Water absorbed by the felt through the beak evaporates, cooling the bulb of the head and lowering its internal pressure. This draws liquid from the bottom bulb upward through the neck till there is a shift in the centre of gravity of the bird, tipping it forward. When this happens, pressure between head and body is equalized, liquid flows back into the lower bulb and the whole thing becomes upright again. But not before the beak has replenished moisture to the plumage so the cycle can start anew. The secret is a hot body and a cool head. And a point of balance whose fate it is to be repeatedly lost, and through loss regained.

The nice scientist with the cookies died in 1969 after I had left London. In due course the university named an annual physics lecture in her memory.

The girl with the golden hair grew up and is living a life somewhere, fulfilled, I hope, by whatever she found worth knowing.

Sister Celestine may still be alive, an old lady well cared for in a sunny convent. If I were to meet her through some quirk of fate, I would thank her for her high-minded gesture in sending us for tea. I might also ask her if she had known about the dipping bird all along. "The liquid in the glass," I would say, "was red, but do you remember what it was called?"

10

Meccano

Strathmeyer Street, east of Adelaide and north of Cheapside, was two blocks long and unremarkable.

The houses on both blocks, built just after the war in what must have been an early flurry of suburban development, were modest working-class boxes with driveways, lawns and fenced backyards. Each house had a concrete front porch. Each had a milk box. Most had TV antennas, some fixed, some rotatable by an electric motor up the mast.

Almost every house had one or two children. Some had dogs. There was almost no traffic on the street, owing perhaps to its obscurity, and so the roadway and adjacent lawns and porches were, for us, an extended playground. We played road hockey and rode our bikes up and down, and read each other's comic books on hot days in what shade there was. At twilight we played hide-and-seek till it was time to go in.

Only one house had no children and that was next door to ours. Old Mr. Innes who lived there was a retired hardware merchant whom we seldom saw because he almost never came outside. Our fathers occasionally borrowed wrenches or Vise-Grips or unusual saws from the cache of tools he kept in his basement from his hardware days, but apart from that he played no part in our lives. Only once do I remember seeing him actually emerge onto his front porch.

We had been playing baseball. We were usually careful not to hit the ball too hard on account of all the picture windows on either side of the street. In any case, lacking a catcher or backstop, our pitches were generally so limp that a decent hit was rare. But this time someone did manage a solid whack that sent the ball straight toward Mr. Innes' front window and through it.

We knew there was no use running on a street like ours, so we just stood and stared at his front door awaiting the wrath of God. The door did open almost at once and out he sprang with an agility we did not expect from a man so old. He held our baseball aloft in his hand and the half-dozen of us stood staring at him from the road. But instead of hollering and giving us hell, he just said, as calmly as you please: "The Yankees are on the TV playing the Sox. I thought this came all the way from New York." He grinned and made as if to throw the ball back to us. But he thought better of it, so one of us had to run up to fetch it from him, mutter apologies and promise to get our dads to pay for new glass.

On the other side of Mr. Innes lived Joe Yurkovich with his mom and dad and younger brother. Joe was a year older than me and had a huge Meccano set with far more nuts and screws and wheels and axles than all the rest of the kids on the street combined. He kept it all in a wooden box which he hauled out on summer afternoons onto their porch so that he and I, and sometimes Gary from across the street, could make stuff. What we made mostly were racing cars, elaborate ones with fins and multiple wheels and rows of headlights. Sometimes there were wings and machine guns attached for good measure. No matter how elaborate our own designs, Joe's were always the most complex and inventive. He figured out how to make curved body panels, aerodynamic bumpers, spoilers, hoods that opened. He devised a steering system that could be locked for when we raced our cars down a piece of plywood propped against the steps.

The porch where we worked during these summer afternoons was partly hidden from the road by two shaggy cedars, one on either side, so that we built our machines as in an arbour raised above the brown grass of the sunbaked world. From the shade of this mechanical Eden we could sometimes hear Joe's parents fighting inside the house, behind the door.

Joe's mother was German and his father Ukrainian, so it was never clear what language they were shouting at each other. All we could hear was volume and pitch, the contours of anger, and occasionally the sound of things slammed against wood, or glass or porcelain breaking. At these times Joe just kept at what he was doing, looking for the right screw or tightening nuts with his wrench. His car, on such days, would be more intricate than ever.

The trouble with the plywood ramp was that where its bottom end met the sidewalk there was inevitably a discontinuity, the unavoidable apex of an obtuse angle made worse by the step resulting from the thickness of the wood. When the cars hit the bottom there was a sharp jolt which sometimes made parts fall off, and in any case spoiled the smooth flow of kinetic energy we wanted to carry the cars down the sidewalk. This could be mitigated somewhat by decreasing the slope of the ramp, but not too much because we only had the one short piece of plywood. And the whole point was a steep incline for quick acceleration. Not even Joe could solve this problem, though he did his best to design his cars with the inevitable shock in mind—he mounted the front wheels as far forward as possible, used the largest wheels he could find, and tried to get the centre of gravity close to the rear. But still there was that jarring thunk that ruined the perfection and fluidity of every run.

In the fall of what must have been 1962, Joe and his mother and little brother disappeared. One week they were there, and the next they were gone. For a while we saw his father continue to trudge home from the bus stop after work with his empty lunch pail, and then that too ended.

It happened on a Saturday morning. Police cars were not a common sight on our street, so everyone came out to see what was going on when the two policemen walked up the sidewalk to Joe's house. For a while not much happened.

The policemen spoke though the door, but we couldn't hear what they said, nor tell whether Joe's father replied from inside or not.

We were joined where we were standing with the neighbours across the street by a pale, nervous-looking man in a dog collar. His church, he told us, had sponsored the family when they immigrated to Canada. "Alas," he kept saying, "that it should come to this." He stood as clueless as the rest of us, wringing his hands and waiting for the police to get it over with.

Which eventually they did. One of them returned to the car and got a crowbar from the trunk. He went back up the sidewalk to the porch between the cedar bushes and we lost sight of him. We heard banging and shouting and more banging—and then, from within: "My house. This … mine," followed by the sound of splintering wood.

And then silence. The street holding its breath.

Shortly after, Joe's father and the two policemen descended the steps. He was hunched between them and looked nowhere. The three of them moved quickly and smoothly from the steps to the sidewalk and on to the waiting car. One of the policemen guided Joe's father into the back seat. The other stood watching, the crowbar clutched in his right hand.

11

Rink

A few blocks south of Cheapside on Elliott Street is a winter sports centre. Although the present building is relatively new, the location had always drawn skaters from the neighbourhoods north of the Wolsley Barracks all the way to Victoria Street. In the 1960s, however, skating here was a primitive affair.

Two outdoor rinks sat side by side, one enclosed by boards for playing hockey, the other with a chain-link fence. In summer these rinks doubled as tennis courts, but I knew them only in their winter use. In front of the rinks a stretch of asphalt led to two change rooms in a squat one-storey building. The men's change room was on the right, the women's on the left.

I never saw the interior of the women's, but the men's was a mean rectangle of cinder-block walls and small, high windows covered in mesh. Gouged wooden benches ran round the room. What I remember is not just a tangle of hockey sticks and shin pads and the disordered jumble of snow boots under benches, or the sour smell of undershirts and wool socks, or the bodies of grunting boys lacing their skates, or even the tripping and shoving or the boastful obscenities, but an atavism that went deeper than all of that. Thrust together in the dimly-lit space away from the scrutiny of a civil world, changing from ordinary boots into the steel-edged cockiness of skates, we were trapped in an igloo of raw impulse. Big kids pushed little kids, filled their boots with snow, or threatened to get them in unspecified ways later. It was a world without recourse. There were no adults to referee. Everyone was on his own in a dim chaos of pointless anarchy. With one boot off and one skate half-on, we were caught in a circle of some masculine hell.

Except that the room did have an exit.

A short corridor led to a metal door that opened onto the winter cold and the tarmac that led to the rinks. The act of stepping onto the ice was always, for me, a most wonderful moment of transformation. After plodding across asphalt on the tips of skates there was suddenly only a worn four-by-four separating solid ground from a white surface where skaters flowed past, their blades drawn across ice with a clean clash and sweep. Legs and arms and bodies leaned into a blur as they swept past. A small step and a push, and then you yourself were launched into the smooth glide as it carried you off down the first long side.

Over all the winters of my childhood I only remember ever skating one way: counter-clockwise round the rink. The whole crowd of young and old, good skaters and bad, all skated in the same direction. People passed each other for sure, single skaters weaving in and out among groups of schoolgirls holding hands, and they curved carefully around little kids who had fallen down, but the motion was an unbroken circling, the whole rink turning constantly left and left as if we were one continuous woven loop. Loud-speakers played *The Blue Danube* endlessly.

There were the girls, of course, with their brown eyes and freckles and wool sweaters and toques. Ponytails swung with their stride as they placed their white skates just so, one carefully in front of the other. They wore mittens in which the round flat part containing their fingers was always extended, like a flipper. In all those years I never once saw a girl with her mittens curled into a fist. Even on the rare occasion when one of them fell and got deftly to her feet, she swept the snow from her tights with a hand fully extended inside her mitten as if it were a tortoiseshell brush. Their movements too, as they skated, were purely in the legs, the upper parts of their bodies moving always with a stately reticence, a reserved grace that rendered my own more vigorous exertions, as I wove in and out among them, awkward and visceral, however much devoid of deliberate bravura.

That fine counter-clockwise swirl always had an inherent flaw, however. Regardless of whether one went early or late, on a weekday or weekend, somewhere on the sheet of ice there was, inevitably, at least one gaping gouge. Often it was no more than a few inches long or a mere inch or so deep, but enough to catch the blade of a skate and send you sprawling. The secret, which the whole circling crowd (except the very little kids who spent most of their time on all fours anyway) understood, was to find out where the crack was on the first circuit and then to avoid it. As we skated round and round, as the pucks whacked into the boards of the adjacent hockey rink, we all knew as one body where the flaw was, and the exact moment to swerve or to step lightly over it.

There's a crack in everything, Leonard Cohen might have sung—had it been the kind of song they would have played at a rink, had he written it yet. But we knew the next line anyway, circling in our scarves and mitts and toques round those cold orbits: *That's how the light gets in.*

12

River

North of Huron, Adelaide Street dips gently downhill onto the shallow floodplain of the North Thames, crosses the river, and rises again toward what were at one time new subdivisions north of the city. Immediately across the bridge and not easily visible to passing traffic, a dirt road led in those days down to a bench of scrub trees and bush by the river. It was the kind of track that spoke of an absence of municipal sanction, or certainly of intent—just a lane of packed dirt formed by use.

Once on the bench the track branched into several narrow loops that came together again among the bushes to form broader junctions where a vehicle could turn around. In places the tire tracks disappeared into puddles that stretched for many yards and covered the full width of the roadway. Even in the heat of summer, these puddles remained deep with brown water.

It was obvious the place came alive after dark as a hangout for teenagers to park and play their radios, to rev engines and to neck. Or maybe to drink beer and fight.

The summer I rode my bicycle to this spot along the river I was just thirteen. I had never witnessed these evening gatherings and could do no more than imagine what might go on. School dances were traumatic enough, but the rituals that must be enacted on Saturday nights by the river—engines and radios and girls' voices in the dark, headlights shutting off among the trees—seemed both incomprehensible and somewhat sinister. It was mystery enough to ponder the aftermath by daylight.

How to explain the pattern of tracks and roadways? Nobody had planned this scrubby terrain. It had come about by chance through the random steering of sweaty boys on summer nights, weaving and lurching through the ruts, left hand casual on the wheel, right arm around a girl.

And what about the puddles? How to explain an eight-foot pool of brackish water in the middle of the track? What brutish spinning of tires, what unimaginable traffic excavates such a hole? And not just one car surely, but an action repeated by many. Not deliberately, because what would be the point? But if not, then what by-product of whatever went on here at night, what commonality of impulse could create such holes, such unreadable topography?

The river, at least, made more sense. It flowed by the spot with an indifferent detachment, with a logic uncomplicated by the unknown. But that too was deceptive. I had never seen a mountain river—water responding with clear trustworthiness to the tug of gravity, its madcap descent exactly what it looked like: transparent, sunlit, flamboyant in its innocence. The Thames was nothing like that. It flowed by with an invisible momentum, a murky continuity that appeared to have nothing to do with gravity, with the simplicities of cause and effect. It felt laboured, a flow that happened because it was destined to happen, to go on.

I might have felt differently about it had the banks been clearly visible, but in all these undeveloped outskirts north of the city the Thames passed through thick maple scrub that gave no vistas or riverscapes. It only vaguely contained an indistinct passage of brown water.

Which did not stop me from longing for and seeking out a clearer visual idea of the Thames. Starting at the far end of the muddy clearings made by the teenagers, a faint walking path set off upstream along the north bank of the river. The existence of this path implied that a passage could be had upriver, not to the source of course, but at least to some clearer stretch of water where the river might present itself not as a sullen passage but as something approaching a wilder ideal.

In reality it did not work out so. I kept coming back to this path all summer and followed it a little farther upstream each time, but each time was turned back by the terrifying tangle of the riverbank. The path was barely discernible in places, and dipped down into transverse ditches clogged with branches or with burdock and thistle, or else a dark green shiny foliage that was surely poison ivy. There were wasps and mosquitoes, and unimaginably slimy amphibians among the undergrowth. And the river, far from becoming more comprehensible, was less visible the farther along the path I dared go. More and more it ceased to be flowing water and became simply a murky presence slipping by beyond the muddy thickets of appalling vegetation.

I am amazed now that I kept going back to the path week after week. Did I believe that if I could only make it far enough I would break through to some cleansed Platonic stream? Or was it the horror of the place itself that was the attraction?

My friend Marcel might have helped figure it out, but we didn't see much of each other that summer. We had both finished Grade 8 but he was in fact a year older, having missed a year of school because of injuries he received in a house fire in Yugoslavia before his family came to Canada. For that reason, because he was older, but perhaps also because he had experienced more of life, he always understood just a little more about the things that seemed mysterious to me. Like why we were both afflicted with pimples, or why your nipples felt strange when you wore a dress shirt, or why Evelyn Loubert, who had been a gangly and irritating show-off at the beginning of the school year made me feel tingly when she got off the school bus the last weeks before the holidays.

Marcel might have known what to make of the horrible attraction of the north branch of the Thames, just as he might have helped me understand the events of the next few years—the dark, muddy river of high school. But we lived in subdivisions too far from each other to keep in touch that summer, and our lives were growing differently and apart. And sometime in August Marcel died.

I heard, too late to attend his funeral, that he had fallen down the basement steps in their house. Perhaps he had had a dizzy spell, or perhaps he had lost his nerve briefly at the head of the stairs as a result of his childhood accident. There must have been a logic to what happened of course. But whatever it was, it had killed him.

Logic, I realized, has that drawback. At least the con-fused tangle of a floodplain, the mysteries of the passage of time that terrify us, do not. The incomprehensible may not save us in the end, but it can, in its way, carry us through.

13

Shelter

A few blocks east of Adelaide, Dundas Street runs along the north edge of the Western Fair Grounds. Maps call the fifteen or so acres of barns, parking lots, exhibition buildings and racetrack Queens Park, and to be sure there is a park-like patch of trees and grass by the Quebec Street entrance, but everyone in London knew it only as the Western Fair.

The fair itself, which lasted a week each August and which had been in existence since time immemorial, was no different from late-summer exhibitions anywhere across the country: Barns of sheep and rabbits and 4H calves tended by kids from farms out in the townships, rows of tractors and agricultural machinery of unclear purpose, midway rides and their twirling neon, carnie booths and shooting galleries and roulette wheels, even a freak show some years with the promise of either a tattooed or a bearded lady, pavilion after pavilion of home pickling and baking, quilting and photography, giant zucchinis, water-colour sketches, lacquered gourds. An automotive building filled with motorcycles and hot rods under floodlights, their chrome exhausts and gold-flecked flames gleaming. And one year Miss Supertest, the big plywood and aluminum speedboat that had established the world water-speed record for Canada in 1957 and held it for several weeks.

Crowds poured in from across the city. The afternoons were hot and dusty, evenings filled with noise and sweat. People ate popcorn and candy floss and drank warm Orange Crush. Teenagers with Brylcreemed hair and the pointed handles of combs sticking out of hip pockets sauntered down the midway, their dates' arms around their waists. The girls hugged pink plush animals. Toddlers slept in strollers and women in print dresses yelled at older kids to "get over here, right now," while their husbands tried to shoot BBs through the centres of aces of hearts. Men with ties and rolled shirtsleeves yelled into microphones to extol the virtues of Teflon, or of a miracle gadget that could not only core an apple and peel a potato but also slice a hard-boiled egg into perfect rounds every time.

None of this needs to be explained. Summer fairs were like this everywhere, and in some measure still are. The hot rods are gone, Miss Supertest has vanished from public memory, and there are probably fewer jars of home pickling. But the same formless mix of human aggregation Bruegel knew carries on—those alternative universes of the rural and urban, of the wholesome and tawdry, and the glorious vulgarity of their seamless overlap.

What is gone, I'm sure, is the one unifying thrill of that

era that everyone who attended the Western Fair looked forward to: The All-Electric Dream Home.

Every year in the late 1950s and early 1960s a three-bedroom house was built on the fairgrounds near the grassy main entrance. It modelled the absolute latest advances in trouble-free suburban living. Tickets were sold, and at the end of the fair someone won the house and could have it moved to a lot of their choice in one of the new subdivisions north or west of town.

From the first morning, lines formed outside the house and lengthened during the week of the fair. We waited sometimes for more than an hour to inch forward till we could enter the front door and slowly make our way across plastic runners between rope cordons through the furnished house. The rooms were heated with electric baseboards, there was built in air-conditioning, a TV and HI-FI in the living room, automatic washing machine and dryer, fluorescent lights above the mirror in the bathroom, and who knows what else. The final goal of this slow procession was the kitchen. There the latest Frigidaire sparkled with chrome. The electric stove and oven worked with push-buttons. There were pastel cupboards and counters and a swing door to the dining room, and on every countertop the electric gadgets of tomorrow: cake mixers, pressure cookers, electric frying pans, toasters guaranteed not to burn white bread, electric can openers and whipped-cream dispensers. Here was the dream—the all-electric inner heart of the future.

Each year someone won the house, and each year thousands of the rest of us did not. But nobody minded, for it was the pilgrimage itself that mattered—a vision of the bright, clean, push-button way things would be for all of us before long. It was what brought everything else at the fair into focus.

One year, however, the All-Electric Dream Home was displaced as the centre of attention by something else. The house was still there and still offered its tickets, but right next to it someone had built a different dwelling: a fallout shelter, where the lines were longer and people more curious.

The concrete block structure was a cube about nine feet on each side and we were led to understand that, while it was displayed out in the open on the grass, it was meant to be constructed underground in our basements. We were allowed in two or three people at a time through a low metal door. Inside there were wooden bunks and a table and chair, shelves with canned food, a box of batteries, a chemical toilet and some kind of air filtering system near the top of one wall. On the table was a deck of cards.

When we came out, we were given a pair of brochures. One had detailed construction plans with lists of materials and dimensions, the other explained the reasons for needing a shelter. A nuclear attack on Detroit (an obvious target because of the auto industry) would send a cloud of radioactive dust downwind straight toward London. From the time of the blast we would have about an hour or an hour and a half to enter our shelter and seal the entrance. Then we would have to stay inside, living only on the food and water stored within, for fourteen days. That was the minimum time for the initial radiation to have subsided to a level safe enough for us to come out.

There would, of course, be no electricity, but radio broadcasts would continue, powered by emergency generators, to give instructions on what to do next. Hence the need for a supply of batteries.

There was no question of our family being able to afford such a shelter. For a time, however, I became obsessed with the need. I wandered around our basement wondering how we might improvise a shelter in the hour and a half available. There were boxes we could move to the corner that was deepest underground, and furniture could be positioned in the room above that corner. We would never have enough canned food in the house for two weeks, but depending on the season there was sometimes a supply of my mother's peach and apricot preserves. I made inventories of what the fruit cellar under the porch could provide.

The nuclear attack drill we had at school didn't help reassure anyone. It was the time of the Cuban Missile Crisis. Air-raid sirens went off across the city and we had to practise running home to see how long it would take. A few days later we were given letters to take to neighbours asking them to sign an agreement that if the attack came when our parents were at work the neighbours would look after us. What that looking after was supposed to consist of I can't remember.

The radio was a problem. We had only a normal radio plugged into the wall in the living room, but of course there would be no electricity. So I saved up my allowance and bought a transistor radio. These weren't entirely novelties by then—most kids had one already in elementary school and they brought them from home during the World Series to hide in their desks with wires running up their sleeves attached to little earphones. I had never been able to afford one till now.

The radio was small and squat with a hard plastic case that said it had six transistors. Two little wheels on top changed the tuning and the volume. The whole thing fit into a brown leather cover with cut-outs for the wheels and concentric circles of holes pierced in the leather for the speaker.

Kennedy and Khrushchev were still staring each other down, but I felt considerably comforted. When the bombs came we might not have a proper shelter to hide in, but at least I had a radio and someone would tell us what to do.

After a few weeks Detroit was still cranking out Chevrolets and there had been no need for the radio. So I started listening to it just like every other teenager. I discovered Paul Anka and Elvis and the Everly Brothers and the whole pulsing tangle of the music of the day. It would be fitting to say that it was on this radio that I first heard "Blowin' in the Wind," but I can't say that for sure.

The end of this story actually takes place thirty years later. I am driving one evening from my house to the little general store a few miles up the road to buy milk. We live in the country and the road passes through fields and forest. For most of the way there are no other houses, and the night is lovely with a big sweep of stars overhead. I am listening to Brahms on the radio. My wife is at home putting the children to bed.

I see a light in the sky—white and unusually bright. It is moving very fast from the north exactly due south. It is not an airplane—we are not on the flight path of any long-distance jets and it is too high up to be heading for the local airport (which is in the wrong direction anyway). It can't be a satellite because they move west to east. So, what? What is to the north of us? The Yukon and then, over the Pole, Russia. What is to the south? Vancouver, and then Seattle. And Boeing and Microsoft.

But this is ridiculous. Gorbachev is President in the USSR, and the world is not the same place it once was. There is no danger of nuclear war anymore.

Still, there is that light moving overhead.

How long was it again—an hour, an hour and a half?

What do we have in the house—a side of lamb in the freezer, a cellar full of wine, and how many days' worth of granola? Which corner of the basement is deepest and could I move the sofa above it, and do we have time to fill jugs of water, and what is this insanity anyway after all this time? This is the future, not the past. I am an adult, I have children. I live in northern British Columbia where life makes sense. The only things that interrupt the natural order, that mar the landscape here are clearcuts and the odd power line.

There are no lights across the fields tonight and no other cars on the road. Whatever is heading south among the stars disappears from sight. The store closes at eight o'clock. I crank the window shut, turn the volume up on Brahms, and drive into the night.

14

Perpetual Motion

When it leaves downtown, Wellington Street crosses beneath the CN tracks through an underpass. It emerges on the south side between what was once the Friar's Cellar on the right and the old Simpson's warehouse on the left, though after all these years neither the buff brick warehouse nor the restaurant remain as they were.

Simpson's is gone for good, both the warehouse and the department store that once tied downtown together at the corner of Dundas and Richmond; swallowed more than thirty years ago into the anonymity of Sears. How long the Friar's Cellar survived I have no way of knowing. I never did get a look inside, my parents not being restaurant-goers, and my adolescent friends all being poor. But the parking lot was always full in the evenings and one imagined an interior given over to revelry, touched perhaps by an air both frenetic and slightly debauched. Trestle tables may well have groaned under trenchers of this and that, with tipsy diners waving gnawed bones to summon fresh tankards of frothing Labatts.

Exclusion can fuel the imagination like that.

The warehouse, by contrast, followed a different monastic order. From 4:30 to midnight my father cleaned the empty offices and corridors, while a Lithuanian named Carl washed the trucks and panel vans parked in the row of garages along the north side. They met for half an hour each evening to eat their sandwiches and drink coffee from Thermoses.

Carl had escaped from post-War Lithuania by hiding in a coal tender behind a locomotive heading through Poland into Germany. He ended up in the West and somehow eventually found himself in Canada. Along the way he had (unfortunately, according to my father) married a German woman who now made his life miserable by lording it over him at home, and by appropriating his paycheques and grudgingly doling him out a miserable allowance. So badly was Carl treated that he took a secret job on Saturday mornings. While his wife thought he was doing something harmless like having his hair cut, Carl cleaned the swimming pool and did other odd jobs for a motel on Wharncliffe Road. He got paid in cash, which he stashed away for his own purposes in a cigar box.

Carl also sold Irish Sweepstakes tickets, but lots of people did that too.

More uniquely, he was an avid theoretical hunter. His wife would never permit him to own a gun or allow him the pleasure of going off by himself to wherever it is people went to hunt. But he did write away for as many pamphlets and government regulations as he could get about hunting deer in the Queen Charlottes. His plan was to put it all together into a booklet and then sell it by mail order through American hunting magazines for five dollars. He even cut up a free road map from the CAA so that the Americans could figure out where the Queen Charlottes were. I was supposed to be his partner in this scheme, even though I was only twelve, because he needed someone to proofread his English.

More than anything, Carl thought of himself as an inventor, though it's difficult to say just what he invented because he was always very secretive. I know he did come up with a self-propelled car-washing brush. There were already brushes you could buy to screw onto the end of a hose, but you had to rub them against the car with some effort, whereas Carl's brush planned to use the pressure of the water to turn a small turbine inside the brush housing to make it rotate on its own. All the operator would have to do is hold the brush with minimum effort against the car, or in Carl's case truck, and it would work on its own. It was a great idea, but it seemed there was never enough pressure in the hoses at Simpson's, or anywhere else in London for that matter, to make it actually work.

But it must have launched an idea for Carl because a year later he whispered to my father that he was on the verge of completing work on an entirely new invention: a completely fuel-less automobile engine. He could say nothing about it, even in general terms, because if anyone suspected anything, the oil companies would steal his drawings and destroy them.

I don't know what became of him after my father left Simpson's, but I can imagine him still at it through the years. Night after night he is there among the dripping trucks. Water sloshes around his gumboots while his mind perfects details of the marvellous engine. In the solitude of the dark warehouse he works carefully through his calculations. They either confirm what is possible, or, if not, open a way to whatever might lie beyond.

15

CFPL

In the 1960s the CFPL television station in London was located on Wharncliffe Road on the way out of town toward Lambeth. It may still be there, but if it is, its significance as a landmark is surely diminished.

In its infancy, television was not what it is today. Its modest black and white miracles were neither the fragmented image-storm of network TV in our own time, nor the unsettling vertigo of the wired world. It was a homey medium based on a language of consensus. As a secular form of the same cosiness we knew in church, it was as undisturbed by the time it took for vacuum tubes to warm up, or by the human intervention necessary to fiddle with horizontal and vertical holds, or by the occasional need to rotate aerials, as our sense of communion was diminished by the idiosyncrasies of Father Flynn's liturgy or by the jostlings of smirking altar boys.

There was the larger canon of course—*Hockey Night in Canada, Ed Sullivan, Bonanza*—but CFPL's more parochial fare was just as important—local news about floods and fires, the illness of the sea lion at Storybook Gardens, ribbon cuttings by the IODE, and any number of disingenuous but vastly popular shows consistent with the times. On a folk-music programme called *Hootenanny* dreamy college kids with guitars sang on the lawn of the TV station about what they would do if they had a hammer. On *Take Your Choice* more college kids sat on pedestals behind desks and pushed little buzzers to answer tricky questions posed by an energetic quizmaster.

I was in the studio audience once for *Take Your Choice*. Each week a different community group was invited to the station, and one of its members became the guest panellist who tried to match his wits against the students. I went with the Navy League, and our commanding officer, a veteran of the corvette navy in the North Atlantic, got to sit up on stage under the lights. As it turned out, he disgraced us when it came to his big question: "You are in a sailboat becalmed in an absence of wind. You have an electric fan and a source of power. If you aim the fan at the sail and turn it on, can you make the boat move forward? "

I knew, the college kids knew, we all knew, even the cameraman hidden behind his earphones knew that it wouldn't work. It had something to do with Newton's Second or Third Law. Some of us knew, from seeing boats in the Everglades on *Walt Disney*, that if you forgot about the sail and aimed the fan backward as a propeller you might get the boat to move. But not our officer. He just grinned a big nautical grin and said, "Oh, yes, I believe so; yes, that would do the trick." We nearly died. Though at the end of the show we clapped for him anyway.

Sometime in the mid-1960s CFPL built a new transmission tower behind its station on Wharncliffe Road. They already had one, striped red and white with a flashing light on top, but this new one was twice as tall. We saw them erecting it on the evening news.

A few months after it was finished somebody climbed up the tower and settled down to camp on a little platform near the top. Nobody knew who he was or why he had climbed up there. Several policemen volunteered to go after him but it was two or three days before they could get him down. He was apparently not suicidal, nor was he trying to draw attention to a political cause, or embarrass an ex-girlfriend, or raise money for a charity. The closest anyone could figure was that he was a little bit crazy. Maybe he just wanted to see what London looked like from so high up. When they finally got him down, the police drove him away and the whole incident was forgotten.

I wanted to see London from the air too. In June of 1967, a few weeks before leaving the city for good, I organized my friend Bud and his little brother Jimmy to split the cost with me of a one-hour sightseeing flight. We went up in a little Cessna and the pilot flew us low and slow over the neighbourhoods where we had grown up so we could see our houses and schools. It was a strange farewell, after all those years of knowing pockets of the place from the ground—cracks in sidewalks, roots of trees, hollows worn in the dirt under schoolyard swings where water collected after rain. And now all of this glimpsed from above through a forest of maples, everything laid out in new connections.

We flew over downtown. St. Peter's Basilica really did look like a man lying on his back, arms outstretched, knees drawn up, a spire springing from his heart. We saw the Western Fair grounds and the adjacent railway tracks where a long line of tiny people snaked toward the Expo 67 train that was in town that week. Then the unfamiliar south branch of the Thames, and beyond it baseball fields and traffic on unnamed streets. And then I saw the CFPL transmission tower ahead of us to the southwest, still the tallest thing in sight.

"Do you want to fly the plane?" the pilot asked. He meant me because I had got to sit up front by dint of having thought of the excursion in the first place.

He gave me a little lesson and showed me the pedals and the throttle and the yoke and the altimeter, but in the end all I got to do was hold the yoke. He hauled back on the throttle and told me to pull the yoke toward my chest. The engine revved and the nose of the plane rose and there was suddenly nothing to see out the front but sky. He told me to watch the artificial horizon. After a minute or two he eased off the throttle and I pushed the yoke forward. The world came back into view, but I hardly recognized it. We were at least a thousand feet higher and the trees and houses below had disappeared into a haze of green. I could still see the CFPL tower, but its top was now a long way below us. I looked for the little platform, but couldn't make it out.

So it was as simple as that: a knack with the controls, a steady hand, and a head for heights.

I looked out the front window through the blur of the propeller. The horizon was misty and a long way off, but I could see it straight ahead. All I had to do was hold on and keep the plane level. In no time at all, I felt sure, the land would vanish and the little plane would keep flying, taking us out over the blue emptiness of the Great Lakes.

16

Victoria Hospital

In the early 1990s Vancouver General Hospital built a new high-rise wing visible from all over the city. But even before construction was completed it became apparent that there was no money to furnish it, and so it stood empty for the best part of a decade. It towers above the old brick Willow Pavilion where my younger daughter was born, though I understand that Maternity has now moved elsewhere in the vast complex of buildings that is VGH.

In 1966, when I had my first summer job in London, Victoria Hospital must have been a major regional equivalent of VGH. In appearance, however, it couldn't have been more different, tucked away on a maple-shaded street in a residential neighbourhood along the south branch of the Thames. The main building was six stories tall. It had a decent façade and a flight of stone steps leading up to double front doors at the end of a short walk lined with canna lilies and petunias. In scale and general feel it fit in comfortably with the brick houses of the surrounding neighbourhood.

When the Queen was in Canada to open the St. Lawrence Seaway in 1958 she came to London and, among other stops, visited Victoria Hospital. She climbed the steps past the petunias, walked about inside a bit, stopped in the chapel for a few moments, and then headed off to drive through the streets of London waving to the crowds from her pale-blue Cadillac. Eight years later when I worked in housekeeping, there were still strict instructions that no-one was to vacuum the carpet in the chapel, sanctified as it had been by the feet of Her Majesty.

I was in no danger of inadvertently breaching this rule because I spent much of the summer washing floors on Four North, the Maternity Ward. My job was the corridors and the patient rooms only, the task of looking after the delivery rooms being left exclusively to female cleaners. I did once venture through the swing doors that led to the medical end of the ward when a Polish cleaning woman invited me to drink orange juice from the doctors' fridge. Once through, I caught a brief glimpse of the inside of one of the delivery rooms. It was windowless and starkly lit by fluorescent lights, and had green linoleum and tiled walls. In the centre of the room was an extraordinary contraption, something like a dentist's chair from a rocket ship, with straps and stainless-steel rods and a number of pedals underneath. Whatever went on here must have been extraordinarily violent because the floor, the machine, and even the walls and light fixtures overhead were covered with red stains. I thought this might be blood, though the room was otherwise quite clean and there was no sign of recent occupation. The Polish lady told me the stains were left by a disinfectant they paint on the abdomen before labour, one that is difficult to wash off linoleum. Maybe so, I thought, but how does it end up on the ceiling?

I was just sixteen and rather shy about going into the patients' rooms. The advantage of being a cleaner was that looking down at the floor was bound to be seen as normal and unremarkable. This was a time when it was standard practice to keep babies in a nursery away from their mothers except when absolutely unavoidable, so I seldom came across a patient actually doing anything with her child. Mostly the new mothers spent their time propped up in bed in pink nightgowns, their hair in curlers, reading magazines about movie stars. A surprising number were only a little older than me. I don't remember any of them ever speaking to me, which suited me just fine.

I wished the head nurse would have, however. She was in her late twenties perhaps, a woman utterly lovely in her crisp uniform, a little upside-down watch pinned above the left breast, and hair pulled into a bun under a chaste cap. The rubber soles of her white shoes squeaked across the waxed floor of my corridor. She never did anything nurse-like, like carry a baby for example, or a bedpan. She just passed gracefully through my days on her way to or from the nursing station: feminine, perfect, unstained.

From the main hospital building a tunnel ran under the petunias to several ancillary buildings on the other side of the street. These included a nurses' residence and a building housing the hospital cafeteria. From the cafeteria a complex system of corridors gave access to a three-storey brick building on the corner of South and Waterloo streets. This had evidently been a teaching wing for medical students but had been abandoned some years previously. Dark hallways opened onto empty classrooms and laboratories. The electricity had been disconnected, but sunlight filtered through the maple trees outside and filled the rooms with a gentle green light. Everything smelled of dust and old varnish.

I came here on my lunch hours with another student named Gil Moll. I don't remember us doing anything in particular except looking around, listening to the silence of the place and to the odd echoes of our footsteps. We might have looked for signs of the former occupants— a notebook, a broken test tube, a toque left behind on a heating register—but if we did, we found nothing; the place had been completely emptied. Mostly I remember us among the benches of the laboratories—trying to imagine apparatus set up, Bunsen burners connected to the gas jets, something mysterious and scientific ready to occur. But of course the gas had been turned off, as had the water, and the sinks at the end of the benches were dry and acid-stained and empty.

These many years later I am tempted to remember this place as sacred, and ourselves as postulants in some temporal mystery. Perhaps it was and perhaps we were.

In actual fact, what we talked about mainly was Vancouver. My parents had just started thinking about us moving to the West Coast, and Gil had grown up there. So I got him to tell me all about it—about the ocean and about cedar, about Grouse Mountain and the Lion's Gate Bridge.

At the south end of the bridge, he told me, was an overpass that crossed above the main road just as it left land to arc out over Burrard Inlet. You could stand at the railing here and watch cars streaming by under you, the great cables of the bridge rising into the sky guarded by two stone lions.

When there was fog, the cars on the right side of the road disappeared one after the other, their red tail lights vanishing into the air, while on the left, car after car seemed to materialize out of nowhere, the faces of the drivers gradually coming into focus, getting larger and more distinct as they approached. An endless flow either way, in some distant and mythical West, cars and people spilling without effort out of and into sight.

17

Fencing

Dundas Street between Richmond and Wellington was, at one time, the retail centre of London. It has declined since then, but when I was young the sidewalks were crowded on Saturdays, and the drugstores, movie houses, stationers and shoe stores still defined what was meant by the idea of a *downtown*.

On the north side of the street, in the block between Clarence and Wellington, a narrow staircase between two stores led to a second-floor studio where ballroom dancing was taught. Its windows overlooked the street and in the evening the large room was lit with the pulsing light of neon signs. The back wall was mirrored and an old piano sat in a corner. On the remaining walls diagrams with footprints and arrows demonstrated the rhumba, the waltz, and the foxtrot.

On Thursdays this room was rented by a Hungarian named Mr. Kafka, who gave fencing lessons to a dozen pupils. He had been a member of the Hungarian Olympic team before the war and now worked as an orderly in the morgue at Victoria Hospital. These lessons were his attempt to pass on what he knew of a lost art, and also to regain perhaps, here in the kingdom of the cha-cha, some vestige of a vanished glory.

Here is a little of what I remember of those classes:

The rest position for fencing with the foil involves presenting as narrow a profile of the torso as possible to your opponent. The right foot points forward, about twenty inches ahead of the left, which points away at ninety degrees, the body thus facing essentially sideways. The right arm, which holds the foil, is bent loosely at the elbow, the forearm and sword extending in a straight line toward the opponent at a roughly thirty-degree angle to the floor. It is important to keep the elbow close to the body and in a direct line between hips and sword tip. The left arm curves up behind the shoulder, with the wrist dangling loosely just above and behind the head. The knees are bent, with weight resting equally on left and right legs, the goal being looseness and balance so that the body can move in any direction easily and with minimal effort. The key to this relaxed alertness, oddly, is in the loose wrist behind the head. Maintain tranquility there, behind the threshold of concentration, and the mind and body will respond to the instantaneous demands of eye and arm and steel.

From this rest position, a series of postures and moves, both defensive and offensive, elaborate the art of fencing. Advances and retreats, motions of the arm to left or right to parry or riposte, form the vocabulary of the body's hubris or caution. In Mr. Kafka's classes, as in a ballet school, this vocabulary was accompanied by French or Italian instructions hurled at us from the frenzy of his animated demonstration: *En garde. En marchant. Botta. Balestra. Raddoppio botta.*

The lunge was the best of all—*botta* in Italian, *botte* in French—the whole weight of the body thrown forward on a bold step with the right leg, the sword arm thrust forward, the body low and sleek and fluid. Best of all, the left arm, abandoning its wrist-dangling serenity, flung itself backward in a sweeping, open-palmed gesture of triumph. I loved that sudden opening of the body, from caution to fortissimo all at once. Nothing intermediate. Nothing tentative but that sudden, reckless plunge into audacity, the narrow blade seeking something decisive, and bending, with luck, in a final pliant arc.

Between one Thursday and the next I did my best to practise at home. I stuffed an old pillowcase with fallen leaves, sewed a red fabric heart onto it, and hung it on the basement wall. Between the furnace and the hot-water tank I faced this target over and over, foil in hand, the steel of the pommel against my right wrist, left hand hanging loose. And then I flung it back like a banner snapping taut, the tip of the sword piercing toward the heart under the light of a 60-watt bulb among the joists, the basement filled with cries of *botta, botta.*

I was of course hopeless at fencing with a real opponent, one who cared less about the vocabulary of gesture than about actually poking me with the tip of his sword. But before realism could ruin the sport for me, the fencing school folded. Mr. Kafka went back to his shifts at the hospital and continued to dream, I suppose, of the flash of steel in a world long vanished.

I continued with the pillow in the basement for a time, till the leaves began to crumble and the heart to lose its allure. But I kept the foil for a decade or two, oiled once in a while to keep the rust off, till eventually I lost it in a move.

I never did learn the rhumba, or any of those other dances. The footwork looked too complicated. And in any case, I thought, what could you possibly do with your hands while dancing? What scope for audacity? What choice ever but to lead, or merely to hold on?

18

Buddhism

Victoria Park is the rectangular portion of the trapezoid formed by Dufferin and Central Avenues and Wellington and Richmond Streets. The triangular piece at the south-west corner where Richmond runs at an angle to everything else accommodates St. Peter's Basilica and its rectory.

Whatever Victoria Park may have become since, sharing with other North American inner-city parks the problems of petty crime, drug dealing and other corruptions of its sylvan origins, it was at one time a peaceful few acres of shaded walks under maple trees among flower beds, drinking fountains and wooden benches—the innocent amenities of a simpler world. There was even a bandshell, with an amphitheatre of metal chairs where people gathered on summer evenings to listen to brass bands and to watch coloured footlights come on in the gathering dusk. If the currents of air were right, on such nights music drifted across the city. People sat on their balconies at twilight to listen.

The formal entrance to Victoria Park at the corner across from St. Peter's was flanked by beds of cannas and red salvias. I remember this because there is a photograph of me, aged about eight, standing stiff and uncomfortable in front of them. I am dressed in navy-blue trousers and a light grey suit coat, wearing a white shirt and a tie, though mercifully not a fedora. A few years earlier it had been an inescapable part of the "little man" outfit, but this was 1958 or 1959 and hats as a necessary accompaniment to manhood were already on their way out .

It was important for my parents to take such a picture, as similar ones were for many of their generation. Children of that era remember being photographed in all manner of such costumes: little sailor suits or bow ties, or, for girls, purses and dresses and matching floral hats. The point of childhood seemed to be to grow as quickly as possible into something else, though what exactly that something was— beyond a vague idea of adult propriety, a sense of the safe respectability of walks under the maples and a taste for Guy Lombardo—wasn't clear, nor is it any clearer now in retrospect. Certainly our parents could have had no idea that in a few short years their "little men" and "little women" would be growing their hair, learning to play the guitar, and disappearing to a variety of unimaginable Promised Lands— Kitsilano, or Selma, Alabama, or even to Monday nights in a bar on King Street listening to Greg Curnoe and the Nihilist Spasm Band.

Well, we all did it differently.

At first, I bought a camera.

I wanted to become a great photographer, recording the human panorama in all its raw reality. For the time being, since I was too shy to take pictures of actual people, I worked on the war memorial adjacent to the flower beds in Victoria Park. A metal soldier stood on a granite pedestal wearing the uniform of either the Boer War or the First World War, I couldn't tell which, but a war characterized by carnage and human tragedy. He was running forward, a pack on his back, tin hat strapped to his chin and a long rifle, with bayonet affixed, grasped in his extended right hand. His posture was one of haste, implying both noble courage and sad futility. I photographed him endlessly, silhouetted against the blank indifference of the sky. The fact that he stood on an eight-foot pedestal made this inevitable, as well as symbolically apt. I was particularly keen on cloudy days when the sun was just visible as a muted disc. I manoeuvred for every angle that would juxtapose soldier and bloody sun, preferably with the clouds looking sulphurous and dire.

The results were invariably disappointing. I lacked technique for one thing. Even when exposure and contrast happened, by chance, to be approximately right, the result was still less than sublime. Even I could see that pathos on a pedestal was just a tad derivative.

So I turned to Buddhism instead. It started with a book called *Zen Catholicism* written by a Benedictine monk from New England who had spent several years in Zen monasteries in Japan and became convinced that as a spiritual practice Zen was entirely compatible with the mystical traditions of Christianity. From there I moved on to D.T. Suzuki and all the rest of it. My favourite was a book called *Zen Flesh, Zen Bones*, an elucidation of Zen through anecdote and parable.

I was reading this book one day while sitting on a bench in Victoria Park. My high school was only a few blocks away, and by the time we were in Grade 12 we had some freedom to come and go as we pleased. *Two monks are travelling through the countryside when they come across a woman standing by a swollen river. One of the monks offers to carry the woman across on his back, which she gratefully accepts …*

I realized at some point that a man had sat down beside me. He was in his late twenties and dressed in a sweatshirt, new jeans and immaculately white running shoes. I had lived a sheltered life to say the least, and had only vaguely heard of perverts in parks, but there was no doubt that's what this man was—too casual, too smooth, too offhand, and distinctly creepy. Strangely though, despite all that, he was not especially frightening. In due course he asked me if I wanted to go off and have some fun with him, or however exactly he put it. I said no thank you, I was reading about Buddhism.

Oddly, that made sense to him, and he went away. It was hardly a moment of *satori*, for either of us, but there was an intriguing weirdness about the encounter that made me wonder for a while whether I shouldn't consider becoming a Benedictine.

Gregorian chant came into it too. I was singing in several choirs at the time, one of which was doing Gregorian masses at St. Peter's every second Sunday. I loved the sad solemnity of the music, the way we just let it drift out from the organ loft to echo among the pillars and windows above the heads of the congregation. The music director was a young man from Detroit who was not only choirmaster at St. Peter's but also taught at the high school I attended.

The truth is we all worshipped him. He was a passionate teacher, funny, irreverent, energetic. He once read out two whole scenes of *Merchant of Venice* to us, changing the plot impromptu to an elopement on motorcycles. Most importantly, he was absolutely convinced that artistic discipline and concentration on excellence mattered in life. His mantra in choir rehearsals was: "No Passengers." He insisted that everyone be, as fully as he or she was capable of being, *there* in the moment. He taught us that, as much as singing required that we listen to those around us, and to the other parts in the choir as well, it also required that we listen to ourselves, not only in terms of pitch and rhythm but to an inner sense of musicality. The first lesson I can remember with him was when he taught us—a room full of gangly thirteen-year-olds—how to breathe. How to feel our lungs expand, and then expand further still as we filled the bottom third which most people never know is even there.

He was an outsider: A Methodist in a Catholic school. An American in the most quintessentially provincial of Canadian cities. An elitist who believed in artistic and intellectual perfection in a world that was, even then, becoming the domain of what he would probably have called (though I don't recall him ever doing so) the mediocrity of mass culture.

One Friday in the spring of the final year he taught us, an assembly had been planned for the end of the day. The whole school was packed into the gym, and I suppose the mood was predisposed toward silliness and excess. The choir was to sing later on, but first there were a number of skits involving various teachers dressed in costumes doing comic routines. As the assembly progressed, the crowd got rowdier and rowdier. I could see our choir director beginning to fume. We had prepared a programme of madrigals, and clearly this was the wrong audience at the wrong time. When it came our turn, he got up and first made a short speech. It was clear that he was furious with the other teachers for their insensitivity in whipping the crowd into a frenzied frame of mind through their undignified buffoonery. He told the gym-full of students that we had no intention of performing for them till they all calmed down and made themselves ready to listen to what we had to offer. It was a gamble, but it worked, at least after a fashion. When he stood in front of us with his hands raised we knew that we at least had a chance to do the music justice and to have our singing taken seriously.

There was hell to pay afterwards, of course, but he stood his ground. The school owed it to his choir, who had worked hard, to listen to the music with respect. Some in the choir were embarrassed, but most of us were with him. For me it was the most important thing I learned in high school: that some things matter, and when they do it is incumbent on us to do what is necessary to attend to them.

Should I care that there were rumours about his private life, even while he was still working, and many more after he left? That he was having an affair with a soprano from the church choir? That she was a married woman and took voice lessons from him late at night in his apartment on the top floor of the rectory? Or that simultaneously he was taking an inordinate interest in a blond tenor from the high school?

I had given up photography by then. Soon I moved beyond Buddhism too. But I kept the copy of *Zen Flesh, Zen Bones* for many years.

… As they continue their journey, the other monk is furious. "How could you do it?" he asks, "Don't you know we have sworn an oath never to touch women, and you carried her on your back." "Ah," says the first monk, "When we crossed the river and reached the other bank I put her down. You have been carrying her ever since."

19

Eucharist

A two-storey brick building on a bench of land just south of the confluence of the North and South Thames housed something called HMCS *Prevost.* It is hard to imagine anything less ship-like, tucked among the maple trees in one of Canada's least maritime cities. But there it sat, with its parking lot and flagpole and commanding view of the sluggish brown water of the forks of the river.

The Thames here, as anywhere along its length, was noticeably undisturbed by marine traffic. Of course everyone knew about the one great nautical disaster in the river's history when a pleasure steamer full of holidaymakers heading downriver to a picnic capsized when everyone on board thronged to starboard to witness something on shore. But that was well before the War, and, except for the considerable loss of life, sounded in the telling like pure Leacock. The pleasure steamers had been history for a long time.

HMCS *Prevost* contained a large indoor parade ground,

some classrooms and offices, and, in the basement, a pair of four-inch guns salvaged from a scrapped First World War destroyer. The guns were housed in their original turret and sat cleaned and oiled under the fluorescent lights of a high ceiling. They pointed toward a little row of basement windows at the top of the outside wall. Through these windows the guns maintained a brave but only symbolic vigilance over water.

Once in a while a squad of Navy League cadets was brought downstairs to look at the guns. An officer who had seen duty in the North Atlantic gave a lecture about the difficulties of ordnance use at sea. There was the noise of the guns, of course, and the motion of the ship and the heat from the repeated firings. But the greatest challenge, he told us, was loading shells into the breech without losing a hand. As soon as the smoking casing from the last round had fallen from the rear of the gun, a new shell had to be rammed in by one of the gunners. The moment the shell was in place, the metal gate at the back of the breech would spring shut, so you had to get your hand out of the way pretty damned quick. The trick was to use your fist, the officer explained. "Never use your fingers or your palm. Do that and it'll slice your hand off just like that," and he clicked his fingers in front of our faces. He for one had obviously had the good sense to preserve them through the War. He never demonstrated the correct way to load a shell, presumably for lack of live ammunition ready to hand in the basement, but we all had a good look at the menacing steel jaws and carried away whatever visions of blood and severed flesh our imaginations could produce.

Such lectures were rare. Much of our time was spent lining up on the parade square, falling in and falling out, being shouted at by petty officers, and marching round and round practising our left- and right-wheels.

Each parade started with an inspection by the commanding officer who walked up and down the ranks adjusting a lanyard here and commenting about boot polish there. When he finished, he mounted the rostrum at the front and prepared to lead the recitation of the Lord's Prayer. Before he began, however, the Chief Petty Officer shouted: "RCs, fall out." And a dozen of us, including the Chief Petty Officer himself, left our ranks and marched to an alcove at the back of the hall where the pop machine was kept. With our caps under our arms and our heads bowed we said our own version of the Our Father in unwitting unison with the rest of the ship's company until they got to the extra Protestant bit at the end.

I always liked this little time of seclusion. A dozen of us, strangers but for our common faith, taking our lead from the Chief Petty Officer, a red-haired fellow scarcely older than the rest of us who took his job of leading the prayer seriously, just as he took seriously leading us through the hours of pointless marching. When we learned in school about the early Christians hiding out in catacombs, I pictured underground alcoves furnished with pop machines just like the one at HMCS *Prevost*.

The machine was a chest-type appliance of a sort no longer seen anywhere. Waist-high, it had a lid like a home freezer. The space inside was full of water kept cold by a refrigeration unit underneath. Bottles of pop hung suspended in the water from several rows of metal frames. The gap between the frames was just wide enough to hold the neck of each bottle. The round shoulders of the bottles prevented them from being lifted upward, and the glass lips onto which the bottle caps were pressed stopped them from falling down into the water. To buy a pop, you grabbed the cap of the bottle of your choice between your fingers and slid it along the space between the metal frames. At the far left, a transverse passage allowed the bottle to slide forward into a box-like ejection chamber partially closed by two metal jaws. You put a dime into the money slot and at the same time pulled upward on the bottle. The jaws holding the shoulder of the bottle let go and you pulled the bottle up and out. As soon as the bottle was clear, the jaws snapped shut again, lest you attempt to remove two bottles for the price of one.

I, of course, often attempted just that. The inner arrangement of the machine seemed to me a kind of intellectual challenge: the rows of bottles, the permissible pathways, the apparent options for moving bottles from here to there. I tried every possible opening to see if a bottle could be removed without payment. The fact that it never could, that the designers of the machine had carefully measured every space, didn't alter my faith that there might yet be a secret key, a hidden sequence of movements that would find the unexpected liberating gap. In the meantime there was always the fun of mixing up the Cokes and Lemon Limes and Cream Sodas as they hung dangling in their ranks.

I didn't imagine the early Christians as abstract mathematicians exactly, any more than I saw an irony in our little group of RCs seeking refuge from the Protestant kingdom power and glory by praying, with heads bowed, around a pop machine. But I did like the cosiness and intimacy of our seclusion. It was the same cosiness and intimacy that kept me for years as an altar boy, serving the 7:15 mass on Wednesdays and sometimes the 11 o'clock on Sundays for Father Ryan.

In those pre-Vatican II days the altar in our church was an imposing edifice. Two shallow steps led up from the altar rail to a broad space flanked by wooden pews for the excess altar boys on Sundays. Then four more steps rose to the dais on which the altar itself stood surmounted by its veiled tabernacle and double battery of candles.

For four decades Father Ryan had worked away on his holy business up at the altar with his back to the church. The altar boys serving Mass mostly knelt at the bottom of the dais with not much to do except shift from one knee to the other to keep the numbness off. But there were episodes when we mounted the steps with cruets of wine and water, or transported the heavy missal, complete with its wooden stand, from the Epistle side to the Gospel side.

I liked these moments of activity, partly because we got

to play some part in the sacred alchemy of the altar, but mainly because I liked getting the gestures right—holding the cruets out to the priest with the curved glass handles in just the right position for his rheumatic hands, bending my left wrist so he could take the starched napkin after he had washed his fingers. He never looked at me, never acknowledged the service, but turned away and went back to the centre of the altar and the mysteries that needed to be performed there.

Vatican II changed everything. No more Latin, no more hidden rituals at the top of stairs. A new altar was installed facing the congregation just inside the communion rail. The altar was waist-high and looked like an ordinary dining-room table. A wood-framed box with fluorescent lights was lowered from the ceiling above it. The priests faced the congregation throughout Mass and recited everything in English.

Father Ryan put off saying Sunday Mass as long as he could, leaving it to his younger colleagues, but eventually he could delay no longer. The day it happened it was my turn to serve.

We entered from the vestibule at the end of a long row of auxiliary altar boys who took their places in the side pews. Father Ryan, for the first time in his life, turned left instead of right and faced the new altar. He placed his hands on the edge, as he was accustomed, and genuflected. When he stood up he stopped. Before him was the vast space of the church and row on row of faces in the congregation. His shoulders began to shake. This was not like preaching a sermon. He had done that for years from prepared notes, each sentence a careful blend of piety and admonition. They were never personal, those sermons, in the way that his task at the altar was. To see those rows of faces while he turned a page, drank from the chalice, held bread in his fingers was a violation of something intimate, like changing your pyjamas in public, or brushing your teeth on stage. He couldn't go on, but stood there looking out at the rows of pews.

I looked past him and saw the rows myself. I could not know then that it would be less than a year before I sat out there myself praying at Father Ryan's funeral, his coffin propped on the steps between the railing and the new altar, the top half open, Father Ryan's hands clasped across his breast.

Finally he began. He started to read, in a weak and shaky voice, from the printed cards with the English words inserted in the missal. His shoulders shook and he kept his head bowed and his eyes on the surface of the altar. I could see sweat on his right temple.

When it was time, I moved to the side of the altar and waited for him with the cruet of water and the glass dish in my hands. Father Ryan had finished reading and now seemed lost. He stood looking at the paten in front of him. Then he glanced to the right and saw the cruet and the dish and the cloth over my wrist. He turned and took the three steps needed to where I was waiting. He lifted his hands into the air but could not go on. He didn't know what to say. His fingers trembled above the dish.

"*Lavabo manus* …" I began.

He looked at me, and for the first time ever our eyes met.

Then he looked down at his fingers. Light glistened from the cut facets of the cruet I held poised in mid-air.

"… *inter innocentes,*" he continued, and I poured the water.

He let it flow over his fingers and finished the text in Latin. I gave him the napkin and held my left wrist ready for him to return it when he was done.

He refolded it carefully, placed it over the cuff of my cassock and turned back toward the centre of the altar. His shoulders still shook, but he seemed ready for what was to come. He would hold his arms up as he read, thumbs and index fingers forming little circles. He would extend his flat palms above the chalice, and he would break the round host with his thumbs. As much as anyone could be, he was ready for the challenge of body and blood.

20

Organ

I was unaware of the construction work taking place in 1957 to complete the two towers of St. Peter's Basilica. The school I attended for the first six months after our arrival in Canada was immediately behind the church in the angle formed by Richmond and Clarence Streets, but if there was scaffolding around the façade of the church, or if the sound of hammers on stone rang in the air, I simply missed it.

Even had I noticed, I would not have grasped the secular irony of the project. The quarry in New York State which had supplied the original sandstone in the 1880s had long ago been exhausted. The only thing which now allowed the harmonious addition of the towers was the timely demolition of the post office in St. Thomas. It had been built from the same quarry, and the Bishop of London intervened just in time to stop the demolition crew throwing the old stones into the Thames, rescuing them for recycling into the Cathedral instead.

Nor did I know that the bells, so elemental to my memory of central London, were still being cast in a foundry in Holland and not due to arrive till a year later.

The Cathedral seemed eternal to me from the start, as I suppose it was meant to. The arch of the great front door, the varnished pews, the coloured light falling from Gothic windows in the transepts, the statues in their niches, marble steps and marble altar, beeswax and incense, were not displaced anachronisms of European convention but the unquestioned furniture of God's dwelling. Enter a place where the divine is, and this is what it will look like.

Doubt came later, and by a curious path:

In my middle and late teens I sang at the Cathedral each Sunday, both in the big adult chorus and the boys' choir that sang mainly Gregorian chant and other early music. It is probably unnecessary to explain the appeal. Partly it was acoustic—the way our voices filled that perfect stone space, how it felt to transform little squares and dots on paper into the textures and echoes of melody and harmony. There was that for sure. But beyond the music itself there was something more, something I can only think of as transcendent.

Up in the organ loft under the rose window we were elevated above mere stone and wood, the coughing and fidgeting of the human world below. Here there was nothing between us and pure light except the row of organ pipes. The vibration in the air, of both sound and light, the pure metallic arpeggios wafting above our heads into the vaulted space of the nave were as close to spirit as anyone could wish.

I loved watching our organist play—the three rows of keys, the pedals under his feet, and the double console of stops. I didn't know what the stops did, could hear no difference in sound as he pulled them out or pushed them in. But it was the manner of his doing it that was wonderful: The need to move quickly, without interrupting the melody or without truncating the precise length of a held chord. Sometimes he took advantage of a half-note rest, or even a quarter, or re-juggled his fingering to hold keys down with the wrong hand and reached clear across his body for the necessary stop. It seemed an impulsive need enacted in a dimension other than that of the music itself, a rite as urgent as its point remained, to me, obscure.

If that's not the path of spirit, I don't know what is.

The problem came on the last Christmas Eve before I moved away. The boys' choir was disbanded by then and the adult chorus much diminished. The brilliant organist and choir director who had got me into this some years before was gone, and a succession of well-meaning but uninspired replacements had failed to maintain the musical excitement and therefore the numbers of the choir. But a remnant persisted nevertheless, perhaps twenty of us in all.

We arrived an hour before midnight to the news that the organ was broken.

It was a fine instrument when it was installed in 1926, but not much had been done to maintain it in the meantime and an electrical fault had apparently knocked out the transformer that powered the bellows. The odd thing was that the transformer was located not in the church but in the basement of a restaurant on the other side of Richmond Street. Electricians were supposedly working on it, but whether they would get it going in time for Midnight Mass was doubtful.

We did what we could. The choir director stood in front of the mute organ and led us *a cappella* as the mass started. I don't know what the congregation must have heard— something thin and remote and inconsequential no doubt. For our part, we did our best, but we lacked conviction. We sang the right notes but they seemed to go nowhere.

Then, just past the Offertory, we heard something from behind the organ pipes. It was the bellows starting up. It sounded like a cross between an airplane propeller just getting going and an asthmatic caught in a fit of coughing. But there was no doubting the electricians must have fixed the transformer and the organ was once again working.

We hauled out our best music and got ready for the communion motet. The director sat down at the organ and grinned at us. We poked each other in the ribs in high spirits. When the time came we were really going to let them have it. Redeem the insipid beginning; redeem the lot.

I don't remember what the piece was. Not Handel, but possibly something from a Bach cantata. Whatever it was it started with a big bashing chord on the organ and an equally big unison chord from us. I remember the director with his fingers in the air above the keys and his eyebrows raised, that wonderful final moment before the downbeat, the last lingering instant before we would blow them out of their pews. And then the crash, and us giving it everything we had.

Who knows what the congregation thought, that sea of white faces turned upward in sudden alarm, or what the startled priests and altar boys must have supposed was going on—had we planned it this way, this glorious chromatic blast coinciding with Christ's arrival in the Eucharist, his Incarnation in Bethlehem? Something to stun the sleepy audience, dozing from too much of whatever tradition had dictated as supper on Christmas Eve? Knock them senseless with the shock and glory of the Nativity?

Maybe that's exactly what they thought. I might have thought the same myself had I been sitting down below.

But up in the choir loft we knew better, knew that it was all a matter of machinery—transformer, bellows, a fine old organ made by Casavant Freres Ltee of St. Hyacinthe Quebec, and us timing the moment just right.

I can't say I made the connection then and there between shepherds abiding in their fields by night and the members of the International Brotherhood of Electrical Workers who had spent their Christmas Eve in the basement of a restaurant. But up here in the organ loft we knew this was all *mise en scène*, not revelation.

We had created an effect, pulled off a miracle of sorts. We with sheet music in our hands and our breaths drawn, united in complicity with the organist. He cueing us with his hands in the air ready for the moment of creation, with as many stops as that moment would require, pulled.

21

Cutty Sark

Two doors east of Richmond there was a white house on Oxford Street onto the front of which a little shop had been built where model airplane kits were sold.

I came across this store and became an habitué sometime after my first introduction to the strange world of model building. A family friend had given me a box with a picture of a B-52 bomber on the lid for my first birthday in Canada. That and a tube of glue. Inside were three little trees made of brown plastic, each with a round narrow trunk, similar branches, and parts of an airplane attached like fruit to the branch tips. And with them a folded sheet of paper showing a long list of sequential diagrams of how the parts were to be put together to make an eight-inch-long model of the bomber in flight. There were also two clear plastic bits that could be snapped together to make a display stand with a pivot that allowed the finished airplane to climb or dive or bank.

I glued it together in one afternoon, a sheet of newspaper on the dining table, and the instructions unfolded in front of me. I loved every minute of it: Here was a picture of an aileron that showed where on the wing its two tabs were to fit into two slots, and here was the piece with the tabs exactly as illustrated. Snap it off its plastic branch, squeeze on glue, insert it where it belonged, hold it for a bit till the glue partially set, and then go on to the next step. No doubt the fumes from the glue contributed something to the euphoria of creation, but I remember loving the sheer progressive logic of it all, the infallibility of construction, the reliable faith that for every tab A there was a slot B.

The end result of that first model, however, was quite dreadful. A few pieces had broken when I snapped them off their retaining tree so that the jet engines on the left wing were distinctly crooked and one of the gun turret canopies was missing altogether. I also did not know about wiping off excess glue before it dried and the plane ended up with gobs and smears of hardened glue all over the wings and fuselage and windows. All in all, perched on its little stand, it looked as if it were coming in for a crash landing after flying through the eye of a nuclear explosion.

But none of that mattered—the building of it had been the point.

And so I discovered the hobby store on Oxford Street and went back for more over the years that followed. I eventually learned how to cut the pieces off the retaining framework with a knife and to sand down the residual plastic, how to apply glue properly, and how to paint the pieces. I acquired little glass jars of coloured paints, learned how to shake them so the solvent and pigment mixed properly, and everything else it took to get the right results.

I built a lot of fighter planes and bombers and tanks. We were in the middle of the Cold War and the Second World War was still a recent memory, so there was probably a reason for all the military models, but I doubt if that was the only factor. These things were intricate, with lots of complicated parts. I never thought of them dropping bombs or strafing columns of refugees. How to glue the bombs on so they wouldn't fall off, and how to position a tank's cannon at a raffish angle, these were the technical and aesthetic issues. Even later when my interest switched to making models of cars, the important thing was not just that the wheels should turn or the doors open, but that the assembly should be satisfying, that the paintwork should cover the seams and that the chrome should gleam.

Did I see a connection between my model hot rods and the cars I saw at the car show at the Western Fair? Well, yes of course. But that wasn't the point. Or if it was, it was only to the extent that the cars under the lights with the girls in bathing suits beside them, satin sashes stretching from shoulder to opposite hip emblazoned with manufacturers' names, were also on display. They weren't useful. The cars weren't anything anyone would actually drive to Loblaws for a jug of milk. They were an idea of something made plastic, so to speak.

Most of us gave up making models at a certain age. Probably the same age we discovered we lived in a real world in which B-52s flew overhead unseen but with real bombs ready to drop, and in which we could drive real cars (or at least be driven by an older brother who had a licence). Also, no doubt, the same age we discovered real girls and the infinitely more complex concepts of assembly for which there were no folded sheets of explanation, never mind all the smirks that accompanied the new meanings of tab A and slot B.

But strangely, I went the other way. At seventeen I bought a huge model of the *Cutty Sark*. It took three months to build and when it was finished it was three-feet long and over two-feet high, complete with rigging and little sailors on deck hauling on ropes. Rather than abandon the idea of models depicting an unreal world, I wanted to build a huge one that was as realistic as possible. I studied what I could about this last great clipper ship, an anachronism in the emerging age of steam, and read books about the final great race with its rival the *Thermopylae* to set a speed record for the London to Bombay run.

I painted the hull with a fine copper wash, tinged here and there with green to capture the effects of the sea. I strung the rigging with ecru thread, dipped the tackle blocks into mahogany paint, and gave the sailors jolly red head scarves. When it was finished it sat on the desk in my room, bow pointing east, a paper Union Jack at the stern. I wish I could say I sat at the desk throughout my final year of high school reading Conrad, but the truth is I did not discover him till later in university, though when I did it was with a sense of familiar recognition.

When we left for Vancouver, the movers placed the ship in a large cardboard box and fastened it to the bottom with nylon straps so it wouldn't come to harm on the way. I don't know why we took it with us. It seemed inconceivable to me that we should not, though I'm sure it added to the cost of the move. So while we rode the train, the *Cutty Sark* made its journey across Canada in a truck. I imagine it travelling westward across the Prairies, in a box once again, sailors turning their hands to the ropes while bedsteads and chests of drawers creak around them.

22

Socrates

For many years the London Public Library was located on the south side of Queens Avenue between Wellington and Waterloo. For a squat and undistinguished three-storey building, it had an imposing presence. The stone façade, reached by a broad flight of steps on the street side, was embellished with a row of vaguely art deco columns in bas-relief across the full width of the building. Narrow windows between the columns admitted light to the tall-ceilinged stacks of the main floor.

Dead centre above the double main doors, a head of Socrates looked down in stony wisdom at the coming and going of patrons. His eyeballs were not shown, or else had weathered, leaving the blank vacuity of his carved face looking like Jacques Plante's goalie mask.

In my early years, visits to the library did not fall under Socrates' symbolic supervision because the children's section in the basement was reached via an outside walkway round to the back of the building. It was here that I borrowed book after book on astronomy, poring over diagrams of the solar system with their coloured balls and dotted lines indicating planetary orbits, and moving gradually to more difficult accounts of supernovas, white dwarves, interstellar dust and all the rest of it.

Some of the books were quite current, though most were decades old, leading to strange discrepancies. More recent books spoke of the probable chemistry of interstellar nebulae, while books from earlier in the century referred to the Great Nebula in Orion in vague and uncertain terms, science having had little idea even thirty years earlier what these glowing clouds might be. Until I was old enough to figure out which books were old and which new (apart from the freshness of the paper and the quality of the photographs, which, with black and white images of stars, often gave few clues), I was unclear whether imprecision was lack of knowledge or whether it pointed to a fundamental mystery, a realm of phenomena beyond the explicable.

My graduation to the adult section helped matters only because it corresponded with a loss of interest in astronomy in favour of science fiction. The adult stacks made the transition easy. Books in the fiction section were tagged with stickers on the lower spines indicating genre. All the science fiction showed a rocket ship circled by the elliptical orbits of a Bohr atom on a bright yellow ground. Mysteries and romance had their own symbols. This categorization made life easy. I started at A and picked out the yellow tags one after the other. I got past the Ps by the time I was in Grade 12 and my reading interests changed again. As a method, it had the merit both of thoroughness and of clarity.

The library was actually called the London Public Library and Art Museum because half the top floor was an open space where exhibitions of paintings served as the city's municipal art gallery. I visited the gallery only twice.

The first time was when I was in Grade 4 or 5. A teacher thought I should start taking art lessons and signed me up for Saturday morning classes at the library. When I got there the class was already into its third week but they said I could join anyway. We took off our coats and boots and were taken into a small theatre and shown an NFB film about galloping horses. It lasted about ten minutes and all it was was footage of flowing white manes and hooves pounding over turf. When it was over, we went back into the gallery where sheets of brown paper had been laid out on the floor, and brushes and plastic cups of different colour paints were available for our use. We were to paint what we felt after seeing the film about the horses.

In hindsight, the intention was obvious, to get us to apply paint in broad, freely sweeping strokes to get in touch with our feelings of motion and grace spurred by the film. But all I could think of was that I didn't know how to draw horses, let alone paint them. My specialty was landscapes. I could turn out very lifelike winter scenes with hills and bristling pines. There was always a little house among the trees, drawn in fine perspective. Smoke curled from its chimney. A winding path led up to the house, narrowing in perfect curves as it neared the door. That all these pictures bore a strong resemblance to the illustration on my box of Laurentian coloured pencils was probably no coincidence. The point of art, I felt, was craftsmanship not originality.

But horses! There were obvious problems with even a side view: getting the leg joints to bend the right way, worrying about the proportions of the head and the curve of the spine. Tails would have been okay—they were just curved paths on their sides. With pencils the whole thing would have been difficult, but with thick brushes and cheap poster paint it was simply impossible, never mind doing it on the floor. And it was clear that a picture of a horse wasn't what was required in any case. They wanted a free, formless response to how we felt watching the film. I would have been willing to try, God knows, but I had no idea where to begin.

How did I feel?

Mainly, I felt hot because I had kept my snow pants on so the other kids wouldn't see my Salvation Army jeans. My knees hurt from bending over the paper on the floor, and I needed to go to the bathroom. About the horses I didn't feel anything. I hoped they got to where they were going, and I was glad none of them tripped and got trampled. In the end, I handed in my painting of a sagging farmhouse in the snow and never went back.

The second time I ventured into the gallery was when I was in Grade 12. Mr. Kersley had kindled an interest in art by then and I had heard there was a travelling exhibition from the National Gallery.

The show was extraordinary. There were the Group of Seven, who I already knew about. And there was Clarence Gagnon and his wonderful paintings of Quebec villages, his patchwork of clear colours and the fine lines of fences and sleigh tracks stitching them all together, his lovely complexities of perspective and depth, the rhythms of a landscape as buoyant and playful as music. But the real discovery was David Milne. The show included four or five of his Toronto street scenes—pale colours, snow falling, the houses seen straight-on without perspective. What made them so wonderful was the translucence of the paint, the deliberate choice to get the feel of winter light over clarity of image, a shimmering vagueness as if each painting were seen through a layer of just barely beaten egg white, a luminosity both mysterious and profoundly familiar.

Once I left London I stopped going to libraries altogether, and began the long process of acquiring my own books. One of the first ones I remember buying was a Penguin classic called *The Last Days of Socrates*. It contained Plato's "Eutyphro," "Crito" and "Phaedo" and a few others. The "Eutyphro" was about the basis of ethics and seemed obscure to me at the time. But in one of the others, I can't remember which, Socrates sets out to find the truly wise man. One after the other, he talks with soldiers and statesmen and painters and poets. He is impressed with the knowledge of each while they are talking about their special skill, but discovers they also talk with the same assurance and authority, with the same method, about matters where they have no knowledge at all. He concludes that the only true wisdom is knowing we know very little.

Forty years later I came across the same book in a bookstore, still in print. The cover shows a golden-hued bust of Socrates. In this too his eyes are blank, as if he were blind. Or as if he saw everything that matters so clearly that delineation of the pupils were utterly not the point.

23

Corvair

On Dufferin Street, across from the Latin Quarter Restaurant, there was once a used-car lot. At least I think
that's where it was. My one encounter with it was brief and
unplanned. On a spring Saturday I went downtown with
my father to buy a screwdriver, and we came home with a
car.

Among people wealthier than we were, this might have
been an act of mere extravagance, like Imelda Marcos add-
ing to her collection of shoes, but with my father it was a
moment of impulsiveness that had, if not a clear logic, at
least a dramatic plausibility. A certain flamboyance in any
case, to which he was not normally given in everyday life,
but to which he rose at unexpected moments.

My clearest memory of him, apart from the hodgepodge
of family recollection, is seeing him leaning against the rail
of a ship in mid-Atlantic. The wind is blowing and the ship
pitches up and down, the sea a mess of foaming grey waves
obliterating the horizon. He has led my mother and me on
deck for a solemn event. Here, at what he has judged to be

the geographic midpoint between Europe and America, he takes the key to our abandoned apartment in Budapest from his pocket and flings it overboard as far from the ship as his arm can manage. He makes a speech about starting new lives and looking forward and saying good riddance to the misery and oppression of the past. It is a short speech, given the spray from the sea and the precariousness of our footing on the pitching deck. But for him it marks a heroic moment.

What this has to do with buying a second-hand Corvair in 1964 is difficult to explain. But we did drive the car to Florida that summer, though it gave us no end of grief on the trip. It needed a new transmission in Georgia, and broke down again a number of other times along the way. Once, in northern Florida, we found ourselves stuck along a stretch of busy highway. The fact that the car was a Corvair and so the hood we had raised was at the back rather than the front may have confused the philanthropic instincts of Florida drivers, but for whatever reason it was a long time before anyone stopped to help and an old black man finally gave my father and me a ride to a garage. After he dropped us off and after we had called for a tow truck, my father went to find the washroom around the side of the building. He came back a few moments later and called for me to follow him so he could show me something. "Look at this," he said, pointing to three signs, one saying *Women,* one *Men,* and a third, hand-lettered on cardboard, saying *Colored* and pointing to an outhouse among the trees.

When we eventually made it to Miami we visited the usual tourist sights: Vizcaya, Biscayne Beach, the Venetian Pool. At the Parrot Jungle, after the photographs with de-clawed parrots sitting on our shoulders, we walked through the tropical gardens. In addition to more parrots, we found a fountain in the middle of an artificial lake filled with fla-mingos. What kept them there, a garish pink flock standing about in paltry servitude to the cameras of tourists, wasn't clear. My father found a tap on a retaining wall and deduced it must control the fountain. Before my mother and I knew what he was doing, he started to turn the tap to shut it off. We realized long before he did that he was mistaken, both in what the tap was for and the direction he was turning it. As he stared at the fountain waiting for its spray to collapse among the flamingos and free them, through who knew what path of amazing logic, water poured down his leg from what was in fact an ordinary garden tap.

One of my last memories of him is years later when I visited home after many years of absence. I had left various items behind when I moved away to university: books, out-grown clothes, photographs. Somewhere in the intervening years he had tidied my things into cardboard boxes and in doing so came across a little book of the sayings of Chair-man Mao. A friend in high school who was a ham radio fanatic frequently received mail from China as a conse-quence of writing once to verify he had tuned in to Peking. He gave me one of the many copies he had received of Mao's book and we had a good laugh at the stilted rhetoric of the Chairman's sayings as filtered through the Cultural Revolution. Nevertheless, I was pleased to own a real piece of contemporary history from such a distant place. I loved the cheap paper and bright red type. I kept the book for the same reasons of connection to authenticity for which many people keep a Bible in the house though they never read it.

But when I went to visit my parents, my father confronted me with the book. He made an impassioned speech about how this is not what he had raised me for, not the reason they had abandoned their homeland to start again in a new country for their son to bring such communist poison into the house. Having made his speech, he solemnly tore the book in half.

I had just finished seven years of university and, of course, found his display both ludicrous and embarrassing.

And yet, when I think back on it decades later, I see that in fact it was a gesture Chairman Mao himself might well have understood and approved. Think of him in the famous painting from the Long March, his face raised to the shining future, brown tunic tight across his proud chest, the little red book raised like a talisman in his right hand. Then think of my father at the rail of the SS *Venezuela* in an Atlantic storm with an iron key held aloft above the waves.

Think of a garden tap.

Think how a screwdriver turns into the *beau geste* of a Corvair: rear-engined, air-cooled, revolutionary. Fatally flawed, yes, and doomed by history, but think of that glorious, jet-black car.

ACKNOWLEDGEMENTS

An earlier version of the preface was published in the cata-
logue of an exhibition called *A Cold Coming We Had of It*
held at the Prince George Art Gallery in December 1997.

I am grateful to my editors, Andrew Steeves and Kate
Kennedy, for helping shape this book, and to Jean McKay
and my wife Bridget whose encouragement and sugges-
tions during the six years of its writing were invaluable.

The book started as a series of letters to Jan Horner when
she was Writer in Residence at the University of Western
Ontario, and I am grateful to her for sparking the idea of a
semi-fictional guidebook.

Finally, many thanks to John and Claire Pickering for the
generous loan of their fine cottage in the winter of 2006–7
where the final parts of the manuscript were completed.

Typeset in Robert Slimbach's Arno by Andrew Steeves
& printed & bound at Gaspereau Press under the
direction of Gary Dunfield.

9 8 7 6 5 4 3 2

Library & Archives Canada Cataloguing in Publication

Sipos, George, 1949–
The geography of arrival : a memoir / George Sipos.

ISBN 978-1-55447-080-8

1. Sipos, George, 1949–. 2. Hungarian Canadians—
Ontario—London—Biography. 3. Authors, Canadian
(English)—21st century—Biography. 4. London (Ont.)—
Biography. I. Title.

FC3099.L65Z49 2010 971.3'2604092 C2009-901908-6

GASPEREAU PRESS LIMITED
Gary Dunfield & Andrew Steeves ¶ Printers & Publishers
47 Church Avenue, Kentville, NS, Canada B4N 2M7
www.gaspereau.com